"Tamara Hartley delivers a
Time Blaming Others for Your
with valuable life lessons to keep ... .
reaching your full potential. Tamara does not allow for excuses, blame
or labels to paralyze progressive development. Tamara's work is a
"must keep" as you can reflect on the powerful insight she shares to
guide you through your own life stages. The subject matter is simply
exhilarating and offers a fresh perspective on how we can view life and
the events that shape our journey to greatness."

Dr. Kim Carter, *"The Igniter"*
www.DrKimCarter.com

"Tamara Hartley combines her wealth of knowledge and personal
experiences to show her audience how to be an overcomer. Her new
book is an absolute must-read that provides not only tremendous insight
into the challenges faced by many people; but, she shares wisdom to
be a champion over any situation. This book alleviates excuses and
transforms the reader from a victim to a winner."

Dr. Bernadette Anderson, M.D., M.P.H.
Live Life in Harmony
www.LifeInHarmonyNow.com

"Tamara Hartley is brave! In this book, she exemplifies what it means
to take 100% responsibility for your life. With a lot of transparency and
authenticity, she shares her heart secrets. They are the lessons she's
learned from the stories she dares to share. Readers will walk away
from this powerful book ready to reclaim their lives and live in their
truth. Tamara gives us a candid up close look into the life of a woman
who refuses to allow her past to predict her future. This book is a must-
read for anyone who has ever felt stuck in life and is now ready to make
some bold moves."

Angela Carr Patterson, Global Life Strategist and
Founder of The Fatherless Daughters Network
www.AngelaCarrPatterson.com

STOP Wasting Your Time

Blaming Others for Your Life

Hartly
UNLIMITED

Stop Wasting Your Time Blaming Others for Your Life

by TAMARA HARTLEY
© 2015 Hartley Unlimited. All rights reserved.

This book may be purchased for educational use. For further information, please write Hartley Unlimited, PO Box 9584 Columbus, OH 43209.

ISBN 978-0-9836373-2-5
Library of Congress Control Number 2015914194

Published by:
Hartley Unlimited
PO Box 9584
Columbus, OH 43209
(614) 653-6684
www.HartleyUnlimited.com

Cover and Interior Design by Tamara Hartley
Cover Photo by Ira Graham

Book Editors:
Misty Starks (Misty Blue Media), Kellie R. Walker (Pen With Purpose), Shyniqua Allen and Chelsea Elliott (CE Administrative Consulting)

Book Readers:
Esther Bythewood, Tia Miller, Steven Hartley, Ajahnay Allen, Emily Allen, Inez Sidbury, Mia Prewitt, Khalilah Scott-Sumners and Dawn Tyler Lee

Hartley
UNLIMITED

For Shyniqua, Ajahnay, Emily, Carl and EJ

---

*"Everything that has happened along the way
has made me who I am today!"*

- Tamara Hartley

CONTENTS

FOREWORD

*You have greatness in you! You are the designer
of your destiny and the master of your life!*

*It is you who will get you where you want to go,
no one else. You have the power to create the
life that you want and deserve.*

- Les Brown

A friend of mine once said to me "If I had to lose something, I would want to lose money, but the last thing I ever want to lose is time." I was baffled. I didn't understand, but now I know it is the best advice you can ever get. Every day, people find themselves wasting time in relationships where they are dying together rather than living together; working on jobs that are far below their potential, being underpaid and overworked. So many people are losing valuable time!

Stop Wasting Your Time Blaming Others for Your Life, written by Tamara Hartley, a dynamic speaker, trainer, coach, and personal friend, shows you how to stop wasting time in your life blaming others for your environment, decisions, actions, and outcomes. She teaches you how to take full responsibility for your life and to take control of your circumstances to overcome life's challenges. When you take control of your life, you take back control of your time because time is what life consists of.

You must also stop wasting your time worrying about what other people think. I often say "What others think about me is none of my business!" Someone's opinion of you does not have to become your reality. Tamara teaches you how to live beyond the limitations set on you by yourself and by others; labels and judgments that can stifle your life and pursuit of excellence.

Stop Wasting Your Time Blaming Others for Your Life is going to save you from sabotaging yourself unconsciously. It will prevent you from looking in the mirror one day and asking, *"What happened, where did the time go?"* This book will help you get unstuck and move forward in your life.

This is a book that I have read and that has changed my life. *Stop Wasting Your Time Blaming Others for Your Life* will resonate with your mind, your heart, and your spirit and empower you to become the creator of your own circumstances. I know it will change your life, so *stop wasting your time* and read it now! That's my story, and I'm sticking to it!

Les Brown
"Ms. Mamie Brown's Baby Boy"

AUTHOR'S NOTE

Have you ever found yourself in a situation where you felt like you were going to just DIE? Literally and figuratively! You could not see a silver lining, rainbow, or speck of light at the end of the tunnel. You did not feel like you could turn to family or friends for fear they would never understand what you were going through. You were embarrassed by your circumstances, and even more embarrassed that you were the one responsible for making choices and decisions that landed you in the predicament in the first place. You were afraid of being judged by others. Afraid of being the main topic of discussion around the office water cooler. Or maybe you refused to ask for help or advice simply because you were not in the mood to hear someone's generic and clichéd advice. You felt isolated and alone as if you were the only one in the world going through your particular trial. Wherever you are, raise your hand if you have ever felt this way or if you feel this way right now!

I understand exactly how this feels because I have been there! Yes, my hand is lifted high and waving in the air. I have felt this same way many times throughout my life. Though I come from a close-knit family and have a very supportive relationship with my mother and only sister, I did not always feel comfortable talking to them about what I was going through in my personal life. I kept many things to myself. Again, not because I did not have a strong support system in my family and friends, but because I was embarrassed and afraid of what others might think. I chose not to share my problems or seek help from others. My family and friends have always viewed me as strong and independent. I did not want to distort or change that view. While I was usually the go-to person for advice and wisdom; I realized that there were areas in my own life where I needed help and guidance. There was a time in my life where I felt it was a greater testimony to appear to have it all together. No matter what was going on in my life, I smiled and pretended that everything was perfect and that I was not affected by what was going on around me. Some might claim that this is a sign of great faith, to live life as you wish it were, and not as it is. While I do consider myself a person with strong faith, I recognize that wearing a mask to hide what was going on in my life was not a demonstration of faith, but rather a façade. And I was not helping anyone by pretending to have it all together, mainly myself.

Then one day, I made the decision to stop pretending. I took off my mask and my superwoman cape. I stopped trying to appear perfect and as if I had everything figured out and as if nothing ever bothered me or went wrong in my world. I began sharing more with my family and friends. Where I was once worried about what others would think of me, I quickly started to see that sharing was not only therapeutic for me, but also encouraging and inspiring to others who were facing similar experiences.

I've come to realize that though we are all different, we share many common life experiences and emotions. I believe that if more people shared their testimonies, how they deal with challenges, and overcome obstacles, their stories can save other people time, energy, stress, anxiety, and tons of frustration. Sharing experiences can provide others with different perspectives, resources, and possible solutions to their problems.

Someone once told me that there are two ways to gain wisdom and knowledge. One way is to invest your own time and energy to learn a particular thing. The other way is through "*borrowed wisdom*," which means learning from others who have already invested their time and energy to master a thing and are willing to share what they have learned. Of course, there are some lessons in life that you must go through and learn for yourself, but borrowed wisdom can significantly shorten your learning curve.

There were times in my life where I wish I had a frame of reference, a starting point, or someone to share their words of wisdom. It may not have completely solved my problem, but it could have given me additional resources to look into; helped me to see the situation from another perspective or caused me to seek out different solutions. Most importantly, it would have shown me that I was not alone and that I was not the only person going through something. And just maybe, I would have seen the bright, shining light at the end of the tunnel.

I have come a long way from the person who used to wear a mask and cape. In fact, I have been told by some that I now share too much information about my personal life. While there are situations I wish I did not have to go through, I am no longer ashamed or embarrassed by my journey. Because I now understand that ***everything that has happened along the way has made me who I am today***!

INTRODUCTION

Overcoming Difficult Situations and
Living Beyond Your Labels and Limitations

Society can be rough! Ask any celebrity or someone in the spotlight who has had to deal with their private issues in the public domain. People in your everyday life, family and friends included, can be just as harsh. You are judged and labeled based on your outward appearance, life conditions, family and cultural background, and a gazillion other superficial criteria, many of which are out of your control. Society's labels can cause you to feel left out, kept out, or shut out of clubs, cliques, groups, social circles and opportunities. While other's judgments and opinions of you can sometimes feel callous and insensitive, it doesn't compare to the labels and limitations that you sometimes place on yourself. Whether given by society or self-inflicted, labels can cause you to have a false sense of who you authentically are. And if you allow them to, labels can put you in a box, suffocate your dreams and potential, and even cause you to become stuck and unable to see your real worth.

I have experienced many different situations in my life and at times have worn many labels. There were times when I felt I had no control over these situations or labels. I allowed them both to define me, and I lived my life accordingly. I believed the labels were valid because of what I was going through at the time, and the decisions and choices I made that led up to the circumstances. As I continued to live and grow, I discovered that my life is not defined, and my future is not determined by a particular moment, state, or a superficial label.

I learned that I am in control of me. Likewise, you are in control of your life and responsible for your decisions, actions, and results. It can be hard to admit that you made a mistake or a bad decision, especially when it lands you in a difficult place, a tough spot, or between a rock and a hard place. While this might be difficult to admit and accept at times, it is, in fact, good news. Taking full responsibility for yourself ultimately means that you have the power and that you are in control. The same power and control you exercised when you made the wrong choice is the same power and control you can use to make new and better choices. So often, we blame others for our problems and sticky situations, to the point where we cannot focus on solutions or make necessary changes. Life is not about being stuck and dwelling on past predicaments nor is it about playing the blame game and being unforgiving of yourself and others. Life is not about going backward and drowning in a sea of *"woulda-coulda-shouldas."* Life is about loving, living, forgiving, learning, progressing, and moving forward.

I am writing this book to share some of the labels and challenging circumstances and hurdles I have faced, and more importantly, overcome. I believe that with every obstacle, comes an opportunity and a life lesson. A lesson to be shared with others and used to improve other areas of our lives. This book is not a complete biography of my life or a chronological account of events, but rather a look at 15 of the greatest lessons I have learned in life. I cannot share my lessons without sharing parts of my story and how the lessons came about. What this book is about, is living beyond life's trials and tribulations and limitations set by labels and circumstances, accepting responsibility for your life, and taking back your POWER to create the life that you deserve! I hope that by sharing bits and pieces of my life and lessons learned that I can impart wisdom and help someone else along their journey.

HOW THIS BOOK IS SET UP

This book is designed to be a book and workbook. As I share my stories and experiences I am going to ask for you to reflect on your own life experiences to see what you have learned and to identify new and better choices that you can make to move your life forward and live the life that you deserve. Self-awareness is the key to making new choices and taking new actions.

Each chapter consists of five parts:

1. My Stories and Life Experiences - Here is where I share my stories. Keep in mind that these are not chronological events of my life, but stories shared from a particular time in my life to help demonstrate the lesson learned.

2. My Lesson Learned - This is where I share what I learned from my personal experiences. Even if you have not had the same experiences described in this book, hopefully, you can apply these lessons in some area of your life and share with others.

3. My Choice - Based upon my lessons learned, this is the new and better choice I made to move my life forward in the direction of my goals and dreams.

4. Self Talk - This is your opportunity to reflect on your own life experiences. Be truthful with yourself about your thoughts, opinions and feelings. If you can't be completely honest with yourself, who can you be honest with? Be brave! No one else will see this, but you.

5. Your Choice - When you write out your action steps, you gain clarity about your direction. You can also better hold yourself accountable. What new and better choice do you need to make to move forward in your life?

I am 100% in control of ME!

If it is to be, it is up to ME!

No matter what anyone else says, does, or doesn't do,

I am still 100% in control of ME!

- Darren Hardy

Fatherless Daughter - *A woman or girl who grows up without the presence of her biological father, due to death, abandonment or absence.*

Fatherless Daughter

I never felt like I had my dad's full attention. Though I know he loved me and that he was proud of all of my accomplishments, he was not there to witness them first hand. He missed all the important moments in my life. He did not see me star as Maria in our kindergarten rendition of *The Sound of Music*. He was not present at my many awards banquets and ceremonies for achieving Honor Roll and the highest GPA in the class. He was not there to escort me onto the football field when I made the homecoming court. He missed my senior prom and my high school graduation speech. He didn't see me off to college or help me set up my dorm room. He did not vet or put the fear of life into prospective boyfriends. He did not walk me down the aisle at my wedding. And he was not there for the births of his grandchildren.

My mother had me when she was 15 years old, and my father was 17. Although he dropped out of high school his senior year, my father was brilliant. He was a science buff and musical genius. He loved his music so much that he quit his senior year of high school after he wasn't allowed to play the guitar in the band. Not the wisest choice, none the less, it showed his level of passion for music and his tremendous talent. My mother, on the other hand, despite the fact that she was a teenage parent, managed to accelerate her learning and graduated early. She married my father immediately after she graduated high school. My father joined the military, and we moved to a base in El Paso, Texas, where my mother gave birth to their second child, my sister Tia.

Even when my father lived in the house with us, he was not present. He was consumed with his budding music career and spent most of his time playing and rehearsing. My mother was the primary caretaker. She took care of my sister and me on a day-to-day basis. My mother was the one who was present for all of my special moments and occasions, as well as my trials and tribulations. Even though I love and appreciate my mother for her constant support, I was furious that my father chose not to be involved. During those years, he was consumed with his career.

I don't recall being overly sad when my parents split up. Though I was around 8 at the time, I understood what was going on. I used to tell people that "we" (meaning my mother and I) were going back to our maiden name. Yes, I was messin' in grown folk's business! But because I never had what I felt like was a close relationship with my father, I initially didn't think his moving out would affect me all that much. It became a natural routine for me to live with my mother and visit my father from time to time. I was okay with the arrangement until the visits became far and few between. Weeks became months and eventually grew into years.

By the time I graduated from high school, my father became heavily involved in the music business. He can play several instruments but is best known for playing the guitar. He has performed with and produced music for various well-known artists. He moved to New York and later to Houston, Texas. We rarely spoke and most of the information I received about him, and vice-versa, came through my paternal grandparents. While he kept tabs on me and often bragged to others about how smart and highly intelligent I was, my father never made any effort to be present in my life or to support me. Yes, he was proud of me, and I knew he loved me, but I wanted and needed his time and attention. He didn't know intimate details about who I was as a person. For him, it was good enough to know or hear second-hand through the family grapevine, that I was doing well in school and that I was okay. I have always been an independent and head-strong child, but I still needed my father.

For many years, I never acknowledged my feelings or considered the fact that I might have issues surrounding my relationship with my father. When I was a teenager and saw the relationships that many of my friends had with their fathers, I began to realize that I had missed out on what should have been a loving and special relationship.

When I first heard the term "***Fatherless Daughter,***" long before Oprah and Iyanla did an exposé on the OWN Network, I was working on a conference for a dear friend of mine who had lost her father suddenly. She had a very close and endearing relationship with her father. Even in adulthood he was her closest confidant. As she dealt with the grief of losing her father, she created a conference for other women who had lost their fathers through death or absenteeism. When I first started working on the conference, I didn't think it pertained to me. As I continued to hear other women expressing and sharing their stories about being a "***Fatherless Daughter***," I realized that I had some baggage of my own from growing up with an absent father. I realized that even when my father was living in the home with us, he was still absent. He was detached and uninvolved. He was always consumed with music and unavailable. As an adult, I began to see the residue of my father's absence, particularly when it came to my relationships with other men.

I was seeking attention, and sometimes in the wrong places. Because I never felt important in my father's eyes, I always needed to feel important in my love relationships. I can clearly see a pattern of me searching for someone who was willing to make me feel important and significant. I had a desperate need to be *numero uno*, and that need often teeter-tottered on the side of me being selfish and one-sided. It had to be all about me or nothing! My way or the highway!

As a grown woman with a family of my own, I still wish that I had a better relationship with my father. I wish that my children had a closer relationship with their grandfather. Over the years, I think we both have tried various times to reach out and to develop and maintain a real relationship. There have been multiple visits and calls. He has met his grandchildren and at one time he even attempted to pass along his musical genes to my children through guitar and piano lessons. But, unfortunately, each time we reconnected, it lasted for a short period, and then several years would pass before another attempt or connection was made. Our adult lives were busy, and our schedules were full.

In a recent interview, I was asked if there was anything that I learned from my father since he was not consistently around during my childhood. I gave this question some serious thought. I realize that, even though my dad and I did not have a close relationship, he did teach me something. He taught me about passion. He was passionate about his music, and he vigorously and unapologetically pursued his passion. He was successful in pursuing his passion and was able to live some of his dreams playing in significant venues with notable artists. I have learned from his example. He was a passionate person who lacked balance. He was unable to balance his passion for music and responsibility to his family. The years he spent in the military were not his happiest moments. He was working and trying to be a family man and his passion for music was not being fulfilled. He was in constant conflict between what he was supposed to do for his family and what he wanted to do for himself. As I pursue my dreams, I make a conscious effort to find a better balance between living my dream and maintaining my responsibilities to my family. I choose to be active and present in my children's lives.

Like many other women around the world, I have been labeled as a "*Fatherless Daughter*." In my youth, I did not know or understand the significance of my father's absence or how his absence would later affect the relationships in my life. But after acknowledging my feelings and realizing the patterns his absence created, I can now move forward. I have not allowed this label to stop me from living my life, pursuing my dreams, or seeking healthy and loving relationships. The strained relationship with my father was not the only influence in my life that I can use as a frame of reference. Because I did not have the best relationship with my father does not mean I have to live out those issues through other relationships, and I make a conscious effort not to do so.

In many ways, my relationship with my father has made me stronger and more resilient. I am more aware of how my actions affect others, specifically my children. I am a more committed parent and human being. I also better understand how I receive and recognize love. While it is still vital that I feel important in my relationships, I have learned that love is indeed a two-way street. I now go out of my way to make those in my life feel special and important as well.

I am not minimizing or claiming to understand everyone else's pains and struggles when it comes to their absent father and how this void played out in their lives. Nor am I attempting to downsize the many other issues and factors surrounding this unique relationship. Everyone is different, and we may handle the same problem in many different ways. However, regardless of the scenario, I believe that we each have the POWER to make different choices and to break patterns in our lives caused by this void. Though I acknowledge my anger and hurt feelings, I choose to release both and not dwell on the past. I choose to forgive my father for his decisions and continue to move forward with my life. I also choose to remain open to one day possibly having a meaningful relationship with him. I am also no longer angry that my father appeared to be more active with the children he had later in his life. I believe that he too learned from his mistakes. When you know better, you do better. I believe he became a more active parent because he recognized some of the mistakes and choices he made the first and second time around. Anyone can change.

LESSON

1

Your Parents Are People Too!

Although I have acknowledged my angry and hurt feelings, I am no longer bitter about my father or the choices he and my mother made. As a parent, I now better understand that parents are people too, and people are not perfect, neither are relationships. I also know that there is no blueprint for being a parent, particularly a teenage parent with little experience. My mother did the best she knew how to do, and my father did what he knew how to do as well. They have each made mistakes and are not perfect. As we grow and mature, it is easier to see that our parents did the best they could with the knowledge, resources, information, upbringing, and capacity that they had at that particular time. Some of you may say, "Not my father!" or "My parents hurt me!" or "My mother or father could have done way better!" We can make assumptions based on our feelings and emotions, but we cannot judge our parents for their decisions and actions because we have not walked in their shoes. We are not privy to all of the conditions in their lives that made them who they are, shaped their perceptions, and influenced how they give and receive love. And like us, when they know better, have better understanding and awareness, they may do things differently.

Many of us have had less than ideal family structures. Not everyone's family mirrored the Huxtables on The Cosby Show. But, because you may not have had a picture-perfect family growing up, does not mean that you are not blessed and still able to fulfill your life's purpose. Each one of us has a unique and specific purpose and our family structure does not dictate or change that purpose.

Though I may not have had my own Heathcliff Huxtable, I had quite a few excellent stand-ins. I had two grandfathers and six uncles who all had a hand in raising me and shaping who I am today. I also had a few friends who allowed me to borrow their Dr. Huxtable from time-to-time. And I had a mother who took her role seriously and did what she had to do to raise me. I believe that God gives us exactly who and what we need to develop us into our purpose. These stand-ins were there to help guide me and ensure I received what I needed to grow and move forward. What we need may not always come as expected, or in the package we imagined or desired, but we always get what we need to become who we are supposed to be.

*The next time you find yourself feeling like a "**Fatherless Daughter**" or "**Fatherless Son**," or you feel stuck and stagnant because of something you feel your mother or father said, did or did not do, make a conscious decision to live beyond your past circumstance, and move forward in your life despite what you have been through and how you were raised. Forgive your parents for not being the way you wanted them to be. Make a decision to set them free and recognize that, **Your Parents Are People Too!***

MY CHOICE:
I choose to release the past and forgive everyone, especially my parents!

SELF Talk

How would you describe your relationship with your parents?

_____

_____

_____

Are there things in your life that you blame on your parents?

_____

_____

_____

What is the greatest lesson you learned from your mother?

_____

_____

_____

What is the greatest lesson you learned from your father?

_____

_____

_____

Are there people from your past who you need to forgive?

_____

_____

_____

SELF Talk

What other things from your past do you need to let go?

_____

_____

_____

Take a moment to think about your stand-ins. Make a list
of five people who had a hand in helping you become the
amazing person you are today.

_____

_____

_____

_____

_____

Now take a moment to send each of them a "Thank You" note!

YOUR CHOICE:

**You always have the power to make a new and
better choice to change your life.
Moving forward, declare your choice.**

_____

_____

_____

_____

_____

_____

HELLO
MY NAME IS

Nerd, Know-It-All,
Miss Goody-Two-Shoes

Nerd - A person who is boringly studious.

Know-It-all - A person who behaves as if they know everything.

Miss Goody-Two-Shoes - A do-gooder, a person who excessively tries to do good.

Nerd, Know-It-All, Miss Goody-Two-Shoes

I am a very analytical person. I love reading and learning new things. Even today, I have stacks of library books all over the house and am addicted to books on tape. I especially love to read biographies; partly because I'm nosey and love to get the scoop, but mostly because of my love for reading inspirational stories and discovering how people have overcome extraordinary circumstances and hurdles in their lives. I am also a professional student. I still take classes at JoAnn Fabric and sign up for online learning courses, simply because I'm curious and want to learn something new and different. That is who I am and who I have always been.

Growing up, I was often called a "*Nerd*," "*Miss Know-It-All*," and "*Miss Goody-Two-Shoes*." I was called these names because I consistently earned good grades, made the Super Honor Roll, and maintained one of the highest GPAs in the class. And I was a rule follower, at least most of the time. Like most parents, my mother raised me to believe "sticks and stones can break your bones, but words can never hurt you." For the most part, I believed and lived by this adage. But as I grew older, there was a part of me that became tired of the name calling. Especially when all I was doing was being myself. Sometimes I just wanted to blend in and not be singled out.

The truth is, I loved school. From the very first day of kindergarten, I was hooked. I loved going to school so much; I would lie to stay longer. When I started school, kindergarten was only half a day. I would make up reasons why I needed to stay at school all day. I would tell my mother we had play practice or that we had a special assembly that required all of the students to stay. My uncles used to tease me and say, "Tammy (*which was my nickname*), you can't go to school today," and I would boo-hoo cry. I never wanted to miss a day of school.

Now I don't claim to be a genius or some child wonder, but as early as kindergarten I showed signs that I would excel in the classroom. I had known how to read and write before I started kindergarten. While the other students in the class were learning to print their first and last names, I was writing my full name in cursive. While the other students were using the oversized fat black pencils, I preferred the shiny yellow No.2 pencils with bright pink erasers. I showed up on the first day of school with 96 skinny crayons instead of the eight large ones clearly printed on the school supply list. While the rest of my classmates were limited to primary colors, I had access to violet, brick red, and my all-time favorite, burnt sienna. My first academic argument was with my kindergarten teacher over the letter W. I argued that technically, the letter W should be named "Double V" and not "Double U." What can I say? I knew my letters and I wasn't afraid to say so! As you can see, I was a smart and creative child with a ton of confidence and a very active and determined mind. Yes, I drove Mrs. Jackson crazy!

Kindergarten through eighth grade, no one seemed to care that I received all As because, for the most part, most of my classmates did too. For elementary and middle school, I attended alternative schools that focused heavily on academics. We were all expected to excel and get good grades. I was slated to attend an alternative high school as well, but I begged my mother to let me attend high school with my neighborhood friends. I wanted to be a cheerleader, walk to school, and to have what I dreamed of being the "*normal*" high school experience. I promised my mother that my grades would not slip and that I would be on my best behavior. She eventually agreed.

Up until high school, I always enjoyed answering questions

in class and getting things right. I enjoyed being first on my timed test and flipping over my paper as a sign of completion. It was a game I often played against myself, and I always tried to get better and faster. Becoming better and faster is the same attitude and mantra I took into my freshman year of high school, but this time it was different. In high school, not as many people seemed focused on their grades or getting into the best colleges. For many, school was more like a social activity with bits of school work sprinkled in between. My freshman year I was in a mixed class that included juniors and seniors. I was my usual self, answering questions and actively participating in class. I did not realize that I was rubbing other students the wrong way until I noticed them snickering every time I raised my hand, and they openly made jokes about me. After being called one too many "*Nerd*," "*Know-It-All*" and "*Miss Goody-Two-Shoes*," I began to take it personally. Forget sticks and stones, I didn't like how it felt to be the butt of the classroom joke. While I was just being myself, some students took that to mean that I thought that I was better than everyone else in the class. They felt that I was showing off, and trying to make other students look bad.

Because of the teasing, and not wanting to rub people the wrong way, I went through a very brief period where I tried extremely hard to blend in and not stand out. I maintained my grades with little effort and enthusiasm. I made it a point not to appear too smart or too eager to raise my hand in class. I started letting others answer questions and put the math problems on the board. I stopped being a work-a-holic and started goofing off in study hall. I was trying to get rid of the "*Nerd*" vibe and tried my best to blend in with everyone else.

The new "*I'm-trying-to-blend-in*" vibe proved to be a very short-lived era in my academic career. All it took was one B to snap me back to reality. I remember that day like it was yesterday. I cried all day. Everyone thought I was crazy and kept saying,

"What are you crying for, it's a B!" I realized that I was not happy when I was not doing and being my best. I was not happy when I was hiding or having to tone down my passion for learning to make and keep a few friends or fit into a social clique. I had to find another way to deal with the peer pressure and the teasing or somehow learn how to ignore it. I had dreams of attending Howard University since the sixth grade when I saw my pediatrician's diploma proudly displayed on his wall (Dr. Arthur Clark, a well-known doctor in Columbus, Ohio). Dr. Clark used to tell me stories about Howard during my office visits. Doing my best and getting into Howard was more important to me than blending in or being part of any group. I realized that I could not change who I was to make others happy or more comfortable. I had goals and high expectations for myself.

My real circle of high school friends, most of whom are still part of my circle of friends today, never made me feel as if I had to change or be different. They loved me for who I was and respected me for my academic achievements. In fact, they encouraged me to excel and were always part of my cheering section. I had let a few individuals make me feel uncomfortable, and I allowed their teasing and their opinions of me to change my focus. For a minute, I lost myself. But luckily I was able to channel that confident, headstrong, and independent-thinking girl from kindergarten. You remember, the one with the 96 skinny crayons who loved school and didn't care what anyone else thought?

LESSON

2

Be You...Do You!

We live in a day and age where many children, teens, and even adults, endure peer pressure and various forms of bullying. People are labeled, singled out and made fun of because they are different. Because name calling is not a physical act, many would like to believe that it does not hurt or affect us and that we can always ignore it. But words can and do hurt and the residue they leave behind can hinder an individual and substantially alter how they feel about themselves.

*I did not like being referred to as "**Nerd, Know-It-All,** or **Miss Goody-Two-Shoes**," and thought the best way to prevent the name calling was to change who I was. I pretended to be someone who I was not. I attempted to change my behavior and act like other people around me. I tried to blend in with the hope that it would take the focus off of me. Seeing the results of my actions made me quickly realize that I cared more about myself and my future goals than I cared about fitting in and following the crowd. Regardless of the circumstances and people I felt were responsible, I ultimately made the decision to change my behavior and try to be something that I was not, and my grades suffered the consequences.*

There are times in our lives where we feel like our behavior is justified, and we blame others for forcing us to act a certain way. No, I could not control others and what they said about me, but I was in control of my actions and reactions.

It eventually did not matter that a handful of students made fun of me by calling me names and giving me a hard time for doing well in school. I had goals early in life, and I was not willing to let their peer pressure and teasing throw me off course. If you have a plan or vision for your life, you owe it to yourself to make that vision a reality, regardless of what is going on around you or those who do not believe in or see your vision. Do not be afraid to follow your own path and be your own person. Don't be afraid to be you!

My desire to be a good student did not mean that I was trying to be better than other students. It only meant that I was going to do my best and be the best me that I could be. You should never allow people to make you feel guilty for wanting something more or something different for yourself. Being yourself and being comfortable with who you are take both courage and confidence, two skills that we can all learn and choose to exercise.

*I appreciate my mother, Mrs. Jackson, Mrs. Leake, Mrs. Goins, and all of my other teachers who encouraged me and allowed me to be myself. Not everyone gets the freedom to shine and show their capabilities. Creativity and individuality can be bridled, and, in some cases, suffocated when people are not given the support and opportunity they need to develop and display their natural gifts, talents, and abilities. If you feel like you are being stifled in your life, I am empowering you right now to break free and be who you are. The world needs your unique gifts and talents so **Be You...Do You!***

MY CHOICE:
**I choose to LOVE and embrace myself and all
of the things that make me different and
make me stand out from the crowd!**

SELF Talk

Do you fear what other people think of you?

_____

_____

_____

Do you fear rejection or disapproval from others?

_____

_____

_____

Have you ever been called a name(s) that hurt you?

_____

_____

_____

Do you ever "tone down" to make others more comfortable?

_____

_____

_____

What are your natural gifts, talents and abilities?

_____

_____

_____

SELF Talk

How are you different from your peers?

What makes you stand out from the crowd?

_____

_____

_____

_____

_____

YOUR CHOICE:

**You always have the power to make a new and
better choice to change your life.
Moving forward, declare your choice.**

_____

_____

_____

_____

_____

_____

Teenage Mother - *A girl age 13 to 19 who has given birth to a child, but has not completed her core education, has few or no marketable skills, is financially dependent upon her parents and/or continues to live at home and is often mentally immature.*

Teenage Mother

O ne of the most difficult situations I had to face was being pregnant at 16. When I share this story in workshops or speaking with youths, I always have mixed emotions about how to tell the story. On one hand, it was a situation that I was not prepared for, to say the least. I was unprepared for the physiological changes in my body, as well as the emotional and relationship changes in my life. On the other hand, I am very proud of how I grew from this experience, raised a beautiful daughter, and managed to still live my dreams. I have mixed emotions because I do not want to promote, glorify, or condone teen pregnancy. Nor do I wish to paint a rosy picture of what it takes to raise a child at such an early age while juggling education, family, work and life. But I always want to be a source of encouragement to teens that find themselves in this same predicament and let them know that there are still options available to them. Having a child does not count you out or predict your future.

I had no clue that I was pregnant. Traditionally, the first sign of pregnancy is a missed period, right? By the time I missed my monthly cycle, I was almost sixteen weeks along! I was scared to death. I was not ready to be somebody's mother. I was a cheerleader, president of my class, and on the track team. I was already looking forward to college and a fabulous career. I wasn't sure at that point whether I was going to be a doctor, a lawyer or Diana Ross. But, whatever it was, I knew that my life was going to be fabulous, and motherhood was not a part of the equation.

It was extremely hard and embarrassing telling my mother that I was pregnant. It was particularly hard because my mom had always been real with me about the consequences of having unprotected sex or any sex for that matter. She often warned me that I was not emotionally ready to manage the feelings and responsibilities that come along with a sexual relationship.

My mother had me when she was 15 years old, and she had my sister when she was 18. My grandmother had her first child when she was 16 and had a total of seven children by the time she was 22. Granted she had a set of twins (my mother has a twin brother), but that is still quite a bit of responsibility to handle at such a young age. Although my mother loved me to the moon and back, she certainly didn't plan to be someone's parent at 15. Because of what she endured, my mother was always up front about sex and its consequences. Being a "*Teenage Mother*" herself, she wanted something different for me. She wanted me to enjoy high school and college and be a carefree young adult. She wanted me to be able to live my dreams without the added responsibility of raising a child. And that's why I was so embarrassed. I have heard from others that their parents never talked to them about sex. Mine did. I knew the consequences, yet, I still suffered from the "*That-will-never-happen-to-me*" and the "*I'm-way-too-smart-for-that*" syndromes.

When I told my mother I was pregnant, understandably, she was heartbroken. She didn't scream and yell; though, I wish she would have done that instead because her silent tears of sadness and disappointment felt even worse. She left the house and went for a drive. After about an hour, she came back. She sat me down and told me that she would be there for me and support me. It was at that very moment that I realized that my life was about to change forever. I was going to have a baby, and I was going to be somebody's mother.

It was difficult going back to school that fall. It was my junior year, and I had to drop out of all of my extracurricular activities. I felt as if everyone was gawking at me. Particularly my teachers, who seemed so disappointed that one of their star students was pregnant. I remember trying to squeeze into my regular jeans and clothes and hide that fact that I was starting to show. As crazy as it sounds now, I convinced myself that if I didn't show I could delay the inevitable. And, I have to be honest, it was weird having a person growing inside of me. At 16, I did not feel like being pregnant was a miracle. It was downright uncomfortable and inconvenient. On top of that, I had a lot of anxiety about how I was going to take care of a baby. I was scared. The bigger I got, the more scared I got. I was afraid of everything. I was afraid of my water breaking, of going into labor, of contractions and excruciating pain. I was horrified by the thought of a nurse having to stick a needle and IV in my arm. But most of all, I was terrified of getting something I had read about in many of the "what-to-expect" books I had read…STRETCH MARKS!

Back then, when a student became pregnant, the alternative to going to school was to get a home tutor and stay at home. I was very concerned about my GPA and did not want to get a home tutor. On top of that, I had several Advanced Placement classes and did not want to fall behind. So, I talked with administrators and my teachers and came up with a new solution and academic plan. I attended school my entire pregnancy. Once I had my daughter, in lieu of home tutoring, I made arrangements to go to school on Mondays and Fridays. I picked up my assignments on Mondays and turned in my completed work on Fridays. I did this without the assistance of a tutor. Many people were surprised that the school agreed to such an unorthodox plan. I, on the other hand, wasn't surprised because I was determined to maintain my GPA by any means necessary.

I was in labor for 22 hours. My water didn't break in dramatic fashion like I had seen on television or in the movies. Instead, my water had been leaking over an extended period, and a regular doctor visit turned into full-blown labor. I was delirious in the hospital. After I had my daughter, I started panicking because I was sure the authorities, whoever they were, were on their way to seize my baby because I was too young to be a mother. It sounds ridiculous now, but I was really paranoid and kept checking on her every few seconds. I double checked her wristbands and couldn't wait to leave the hospital and get her home. It seemed my conspiracy theory and worst fear had come true when I had to leave my daughter in the hospital for a few days after I was released. She spent three nights in the neonatal unit because she had meconium aspiration syndrome, which simply meant she had a bowel movement while she was still inside of me. They needed to monitor her and run a few more tests to make sure the icky black stuff didn't get into her lungs.

My daughter's father was not in the picture. Though we had known each other for a few years, we were not in a relationship, and I had no intention of being with him long-term. I wasn't exactly sure how everything was going to turn out and how I was going to provide for my child. But when I first saw my daughter's chubby cheeks and lips that looked like she had on lipstick, my maternal instincts kicked in. I made up my mind at that very moment to strive to be the best mother I could be. I made the commitment to do whatever it took to make it. I was determined to live my dreams, to do the things I had planned to do with my life, and still be a great mother.

During my senior year, I was again voted class president. I was also president of the National Honor Society and a varsity cheerleader. I continued with my Advanced Placement classes and other academic activities. It was business as usual as I was still working for an academic scholarship for college. With the support of my mother, sister, grandmother, and cheerleading coach, I was able to enjoy my senior year.

Although my mother helped me, she did not allow me to get off scot-free. I worked a part-time job and took care of my daughter. I bought her clothes, diapers, milk, and anything else she needed.

I developed some tricks for getting things done and staying on course. I remember times when I would take my daughter outside and sit under our tree and read my textbooks to her. She thought we were outside enjoying the weather and that I was reading her a story. In actuality, I was studying and doing my homework.

I graduated third in my senior class with a final GPA of 3.976. My daughter was a year old. I received a full-ride academic scholarship to The Ohio State University, but I turned it down to attend my beloved Howard University. I also got accepted into Hampton University and Clark Atlanta University. My mother kept my daughter during my first year of college. She was willing to keep her until I graduated, but I did not want her to do that. Again, I wanted to be the best mother I could be and raise my child. I did not want my daughter to be confused about who her mother was. I was afraid that the distance between us would be detrimental. I took my daughter to college with me my sophomore year. I attended classes at Howard University, and she attended classes at the preschool on Howard's campus. Years later, when it came time for my daughter to choose a college, I tried to convince her to follow in my footsteps and attend Howard University. Her reply to me was, *"I've already been there!"* Whenever I think about her response it always makes me laugh out loud!

LESSON 3

Where There Is Desire, Determination, And Action…There Is Always A Way!

Just because a system or process has traditionally worked a certain way, does not mean that you cannot change it or tweak it to better serve your unique needs and situation. You've heard it said that where there's a will, there is a way. Well, take it from me that it takes more than "will" to make a way. That will or strong desire has to be combined with determination and action. With this combination, you can accomplish anything!

*Getting pregnant and becoming a "**Teenage Mother**" was not in my plans. It was something that happened and something that I had to deal with and manage. Many teenage parents, and others who have made mistakes, often experience people giving up on them or completely writing them off. I was no exception. Because I made a mistake, I was no longer supposed to accomplish my goals or live my dreams. I was not expected to graduate high school, let alone attend college. In fact, one of my guidance counselors told me not to apply to Howard University because the application process was too hard and, in light of my pregnant state, it was probably a waste of my time. She suggested I focus on "other, more realistic options." I was determined to reach my goals and even though it was hard work, I created a plan and took action. Many people thought I was crazy for trying to change the high school system, and for taking my daughter away to college, mainly because my mother was more than willing to care of for her while I was away. Regardless, I had to give it a try, and, when I did, it worked in my favor.*

Never let others count you out and tell you how your life is supposed to turn out solely based upon your current predicament. More importantly, don't count yourself out. Don't give up on yourself or your dream. Never be afraid to try something different or do something in a fresh new way. Never be afraid to ask for what you want and need, even if it seems or sounds impossible. And never be afraid to work your plan. I am living proof that **Where There Is Desire, Determination, And Action…There Is Always A Way!**

MY CHOICE:
I am talented and creative. I can solve any problem and face any challenge when I apply myself and put my mind to it. I choose to apply myself and take ACTION!

SELF Talk

What mistake(s) have you made that has changed

the course of your life?

_____

_____

_____

Have you ever been told that you "CAN'T" do something?
If so, what?

_____

_____

_____

Does being told "NO!" keep you from achieving a goal
or moving forward with your idea?

_____

_____

_____

What rule or tradition would you like to change?

_____

_____

_____

SELF Talk

YOUR CHOICE:

**You always have the power to make a new and
better choice to change your life.
Moving forward, declare your choice.**

_____

_____

_____

_____

_____

_____

Not Special - *Of common quality, rank or ability. Normal or usual, not unusual, different, or special. Not very impressive.*

Not Special

During my very first class at Howard University, the professor stood in front of the class and asked the following questions: "How many of you were president of your graduating class?" My hand, along with the hands of almost everyone else in the entire class went up. "How many of you were a part of the National Honor Society?" Again, my hand and the hands of just about everyone in the entire class went up. "How many of you received special honors and graduated in the top ten of your class?" This time every hand went up. "How many of you were cheerleaders and athletes?" Again, the majority of hands went up. To be quite honest, I was beaming inside. I was proud of myself for being able to raise my hand so many times. And I even felt a sense of pride that so many others around me were raising their hands. I felt like I was in great company. I was back in my comfort zone, like when I was in elementary and middle school, where the entire class was expected to excel. Then the professor said something that shocked us all. "Great, well as you can see, almost all of you raised your hands to many of my questions. You are neck-in-neck in accolades and accomplishments. So, while you each may have been special back in your high school and hometown, you are not special here!"

I am sure the professor meant well, and, while I believe her intent was to challenge us in some way, her comment cut like a knife. Now isn't that like many teachers, parents, and grown-ups, to say things that are meant to test, push and challenge children, but instead leaves them feeling broken and cut down. For some people, these moments can become life changing. That first day of class was life changing for me. While I never thought I was better than anyone, I always felt that there was something inside of me that made me stand out. That something gave me confidence that helped me to excel at most everything I set out to accomplish. Yes, I believed that I was extraordinary. Now someone was telling me that I was "***Not Special***" and that everything I had accomplished in my life up until that point was, in fact, ordinary and common. This new revelation proved to be yet another significant turning point in my academic career.

I struggled my entire freshman year of college, both academically and socially. When my mother, aunt, and grandmother dropped me off at Howard, I didn't know a soul. We did not have any family in the area, and no one from my school or city, which I knew of at the time, was attending the University. There I was again, starting from scratch. In high school, I became popular through my involvement in school activities. Now I was starting over, and I felt very detached from my new surroundings. On top of that, I missed my daughter. I struggled to find my place. And that revelation from my professor shook my confidence.

Of course, I couldn't blame my academic failure on my professor. Even though it would have been more convenient and taken a little heat off of me, it was not the truth. However, I can pinpoint that incident as the push that started me rolling downhill. My self-confidence had taken a major blow, which significantly affected my academic performance.

Up until college, things had come to me easily. Aside from that brief period in high school, I never had trouble fitting in and being social. In fact, I considered myself a leader, and I loved being involved in activities. And for some reason, during my freshman year of college, those things that had always come to me naturally seemed to elude me; even learning. As expected, college classes were more rigorous than high school. The workload was double that of what I had been used to, and the classes were fast-paced. My track record had always been to conquer any challenge set before me and to come out on top, but I had an extremely difficult time adjusting to my new college life. That first semester, I received my very first F. Now, I had *seen* an F before, but never next to my name, so you can imagine how shocked, dazed and confused I was. I cried tears of frustration and disappointment. I called my mother, my grandparents, and anyone else back in Columbus, Ohio, who would listen. I even met with my professor and the college dean. I knew there had to be some mistake. Maybe there was a terrible glitch in the grading system or some operator error. Maybe the professor was typing too fast when she was inputting grades and mixed me up with another student named "Bythewood." Yes, I know what you are thinking right now, Bythewood is a very unusual and uncommon name and not easily confused, but it was still a possibility, right? Ok, yes, that was a stretch!

After I received an F, my confidence was completely deflated. How on earth had I ever made it through high school, I remember asking myself. Was I a fluke? Did I deserve to graduate third in my class? Maybe high school was not as challenging as it should have been. Though I had taken Advanced Placement classes, I began wondering if they were challenging enough. Maybe the reason I got good grades throughout school was because it was too easy. These thoughts bombarded my mind as I continued to struggle through the rest of my freshman year. Though I hung out on the yard from time to time (and anyone that has attended Howard University, or happened to stop by for a visit, knows that when the sun is shining, the yard is the place to be), I did not get involved in any activities. I was struggling academically and didn't feel like I had the time or luxury to concentrate on anything else.

Sophomore year, I was determined to turn things around. I had my daughter with me, and I had begun to develop relationships. Although I was more social, I devoted more time to studying and changed my study habits, which I discovered were not up to par. I have somewhat of a photographic memory, so I perfected a technique known as "cramming." Cramming had gotten me through high school. I never had to study hard or for extended periods of time. I easily retained formulas, dates, and information. It became apparent that cramming was not enough to make it through college. I started spending more time in the library and taking my work more seriously. By changing my habits and developing some new skills, my grades began to show improvement, and I quickly regained confidence in myself and my academic abilities. Who knew that buckling down, studying more, and developing some real study skills could actually pay off and change my outcomes?

LESSON 4

Whatever You Choose To Believe Is True, Is True!

Henry Ford once said, "Whether you think you can or think you can't, you are right." In other words, if you think you can do something, your belief will drive you to succeed. If you think you can't do something, your belief will stop you from achieving. I had always believed that I had something special inside of me and that I could do anything, especially when it came to achieving academic excellence. But that first day of class I received a blow to my self-confidence that made me think otherwise, and I immediately began to fail.

*Hearing an esteemed professor tell me that I was "**Not Special**" shook my confidence and made me doubt my abilities. Then I started questioning my past accomplishments and wondering how I was ever capable of achieving. As my confidence wavered, I also began to question other areas of my life that had nothing to do with academics. The truth is, I was already nervous and scared about going away to college, starting from scratch, fitting in, and meeting new people. The revelation I received the first day of class collided with my existing fears, creating a perfect storm that threw me off kilter. Then I took that one comment and applied it to every area of my college experience. So, when I began to struggle and believe that things were going downhill, they were, and my belief accelerated the process. So often, we allow one comment, one piece of criticism, feedback, or information to change the view we have of ourselves and alter our entire existence. Instead of taking* my professor's comment for what it was—an observation or even an opinion—I internalized her comment and allowed it to become something that I believed about myself.

I lost confidence in myself and began to feel inadequate, and I ignored the real issues that needed to be addressed. Part of the reason I was failing was because I needed to improve my study skills and change some of my habits. I needed to step up to the college level. Instead of using my academic history as a track record to encourage myself, I minimized my accomplishments and stopped believing in myself altogether. I allowed being told that I was "**Not Special**" to become my scapegoat. Instead of putting in the work to achieve results, I was using this label as an excuse to fail.

Our Creator has blessed each of us with special and unique gifts and talents. Even if you and the entire world have the same abilities, you are still unique and extraordinary because you are you. No one will execute and use your combination of skills in the exact same way that you do. My friend and mentor, Les Brown, says that we each have a unique energy signature that makes us special. However, being gifted in a particular area does not mean that you do not have to put in work to develop your talent and continuously improve and hone your special gifts.

We can become complacent with things that come naturally to us. But the truth is, we should never stop growing, learning, evolving, and honing and improving our skills. Gifts and talent alone do not make you successful; you have to put in the necessary work to continue to see results. You also have to believe in yourself, your dreams, your ideas, and your abilities, even if no one else around you does because **Whatever You Choose To Believe Is True, Is True!**

MY CHOICE:
I believe that I am special and unique. I choose
to put in the work and continuously hone and improve
my gifts, talents, skills, and abilities!

SELF Talk

What are at least three things that are unique about you?

_____

_____

_____

On a scale of 1-10, with 10 being the highest, how would you
rate your level of self-confidence and why?

_____

_____

_____

Do you believe in yourself, and your gifts, talents and abilities?

_____

_____

_____

Do you continuously seek out ways to enhance
your gifts, talents and abilities?

_____

_____

_____

SELF Talk

Can you receive constructive criticism/feedback

and make self-improvements?

_____

_____

_____

YOUR CHOICE:

**You always have the power to make a new and
better choice to change your life.
Moving forward, declare your choice.**

_____

_____

_____

_____

_____

_____

College Dropout - *A person who stops going to a school, college, etc., before finishing or withdraws before completing a course of instruction.*

College Dropout

I would not trade my time at Howard University for anything in the world. It was a dream come true for me to get accepted and attend the University. I met some great friends; whom I still communicate and keep in touch with today. I loved living in Washington, D.C. and the ambiance of being in such a cultural and eclectic city. It is also the city where I had many of my "firsts." I rented my first apartment in D.C., bought my first car in D.C., and landed my first real job in D.C. I met my first mentor in D.C., who took me under her wing and taught me how to navigate the professional world. She is still a confidant and one of my dearest friends. Because I had so many great experiences and met so many amazing people while I was at Howard, I can never regret the choice I made to follow my dream.

What I do regret, occasionally, is that I gave up a full-ride academic scholarship to The Ohio State University to attend Howard. At the time, I had no idea how significant this opportunity was. Being a first-generation college student and the first person on both sides of my family to attend college had its advantages and disadvantages. The greatest disadvantage was that we lacked knowledge and did not fully understand how the college system worked, particularly, the financial aid system. My entire family was extremely proud of me for getting into such a prestigious university. We were all excited about my future; so excited that we didn't do any real research about financing my education. While I didn't receive a full ride, we knew that I had a combination of money from scholarships, grants, and aid. We assumed that everything was covered, and they were, up until my junior year when I tried to get validated for the fall semester.

The previous year, I moved out of the traditional dorm into an apartment owned by Howard University so that I could bring my daughter to school. I was under the assumption that the money that previously paid for the dorm would now pay for my apartment on campus. And it would have, had I checked the appropriate box on the financial-aid paperwork. Because I neglected to check the appropriate box, I ended up owing a balance at the end of the year for the apartment, which I did not realize until I tried to get validated for the fall semester. I tried to go back and use my financial aid to cover the balance of the apartment, but could not do so because, at that point, it was considered a "back balance." A student cannot use federal funds to pay for a back balance. I did everything I knew to do to stay in school. I met with the head of the financial aid department, my academic dean, and anyone else who I thought had any influence. I even wrote Oprah in hopes that she would hear my story and help me stay in school!

I applied for a personal loan and was denied. Both my mother and grandmother applied and they were denied as well. It seemed as if no one in my family was in a financial position to get a loan. I did eventually find out that, as an independent student, I qualified for additional aid, but I had missed the deadline by two weeks. After several meetings, my financial advisor finally told me, "Honey, you are going to have to sit out for this semester," and, unfortunately, she was right. And if the rain was not already pouring, I lost my scholarship money because I was not validated, and it was getting well into the semester. Hindsight is 20/20! I know now that I had plenty of options other than dropping out of school. For one, I could have stayed and worked off the balance. The amount I owed was less than $8,000 though at that time, with very few monetary resources, it felt like 8 million dollars. I had never produced or seen that amount of money at one time. The only solution or option I saw was to drop out of school and work full time. I had a Stay-in-School job working for the Department of Veterans Affairs. When my mentor and employer found out that my inability to get validated for the semester would eventually lead to my ineligibility for the program, they immediately sprang into action and helped me to get hired on as a full-time government employee.

I dropped out of school and found a "*real*" apartment off campus, which meant I now had some "*real*" bills. Having to drop out of school started another downhill spiral for me. I fell into a deep depression. Being a student was all I knew. Even though I had a rough start in college, I still loved school and learning. I was angry and frustrated with myself for not having a better plan and for not knowing what to do. I began doubting my decision-making skills. Again, I revisited my decision to attend Howard versus staying home in my comfort zone and attending OSU. I questioned my decision to move out of the dorm and to bring my daughter to college with me. Why couldn't I have left her with my mother and continued to live in the dorm? I was angry at my family for not being filthy rich, like some of the other students. I was mad at the administration of Howard University. Surely someone could have pulled some strings, or done something to help me stay in school. After all, they owned the apartments I was living in at the time. It just didn't seem right or fair. I was mad at Oprah for ignoring me and not responding to my letter. I had so many plans for that semester. At last, I had declared a major and switched to the school of communication. That semester I also had plans to pledge a sorority and to get involved with student government.

I was angry at so many things and so many people that I couldn't focus on any viable solutions. I concluded that everyone had let *me* down.

I continued to live and work in D.C. even though I never went back to Howard University. Over the years, I have come in contact with numerous individuals who also encountered financial hardship. They too had to take a semester or two, or in some cases, years off from school while they paid off debts and/or worked their way through college. But for some reason, at the time, I did not see that as a possible solution. I could not see how to fix my financial bind. Instead, I dropped out of school and became depressed. I lost weight, my hair was thinning and falling out, and I wasn't eating properly. I eventually moved back home to Ohio, which only seemed to add to my depression. Everyone was curious as to know why I was back home and wanted to know what had happened. I was officially a "***College Dropout***."

It took me a long time to recover from this setback. For years, I would become depressed around graduation time when my family, friends, and other people I knew were graduating from college, starting master degree programs, and moving on with their adult lives. I was stuck. I was back at home and working a dead-end job. I didn't feel like I deserved to complete my education or move on with my life. I was punishing myself for somehow squandering a tremendous opportunity. At age 23, I felt as if my entire life was over and that I deserved the hardships and circumstances that came my way as a result of my poor decision-making. For a long time, I wouldn't share with anyone, who didn't already know, that I even attended Howard University. Yes, I was still somewhat proud that I got accepted and went to school up until my junior year, but I was embarrassed and ashamed that I didn't graduate. I couldn't bear the natural questions that followed once someone found out I attended the HBCU. "What year did you graduate?" "What was your major?" "Did you pledge?" "Did you know so-and-so?" It was hard to discuss and even more difficult to have to explain my series of unfortunate events.

One day, I was waiting at a traffic light, headed to my dead-end job, and it hit me out of nowhere, like a ton of bricks, that my life did not have to be the way that it was. I was unhappy, and I needed to make some changes. I was working a job that I did not enjoy and cutting myself off from the rest of the world. For the first time in my life, I had no plans for the future. Things did not turn out how I had dreamed and planned since the sixth grade, and I didn't have a Plan B. Then I remembered that I had been in a similar place before – in a predicament that I had not prepared or planned for. When faced with the similar predicament I had created an action plan, executed that plan, and it worked. I had dug my way out of that ditch. That day at the traffic like I thought to myself *"Can't I do that same thing again? Create a new plan for myself?"* The answer was "YES" and that is what I did. Before I even made it to work, I had created a new action plan for myself, a new plan for my life. I decided that day to complete my education and to find a better a job that better matched my skills and qualifications. I wanted to do something that I could get excited about and make more money. Within the next two weeks, I had a new job, and I enrolled in school and registered for classes. It took me some time, but I completed a bachelor's degree in business administration with a minor in marketing promotions. I went on to receive a dual master's degree in marketing and communications. Not bad for a *"Plan B"* and a comeback from what I had considered an epic failure in my life.

LESSON 5

If Plan A Fails, Don't Be Afraid To Execute Plan B!

I have heard it said that having a Plan B means you don't believe that you can achieve Plan A. This belief kept me paralyzed. When my plan failed, I didn't even consider coming up with a new plan. Now I know that when Plan A doesn't work out exactly as you thought it would, you have to have the courage and the wisdom to create a new plan. You have to be resilient and find a way to scale hurdles and bounce back from setbacks. That does not mean that you do not believe in yourself. It means that you love yourself enough to keep moving and make critical decisions that continue to move you forward, even if it comes to Plan C, Plan D, Plan E, F through Z. Learn your lessons, and turn every obstacle into an opportunity. That can seem easier said than done, especially when you are still in the midst of the storm, but it can be done.

Face your challenges head on. Ignoring a problem does not fix it or make it go away. When you are done using whatever mechanism or device you use to avoid dealing with the problem, the problem will still be there. I hid behind my depression for years. While depression made others initially feel sorry for me and kept them from asking too many questions, it also kept me from getting back into the game and from trying again. I became stagnant and eventually stuck in my situation.

Don't waste time blaming others for your problems. I spent far too much time blaming Howard University, my family, and Oprah Winfrey. I was so mad at Oprah that I wouldn't even watch her show, which was irrational, unrealistic, and plain ridiculous.

Blaming others takes away your power. It also clouds your judgment and can leave you paralyzed. Howard University was doing their due diligence, and following federal guidelines and protocol. I was no different than a million other students facing financial difficulties. I know, without a shadow of a doubt, that my family loves and supports me. They would have done anything to help me succeed. If I had come up with a plan, they would have certainly had my back. As for Oprah, that was a desperate shot in the dark! We often do desperate things when our backs are against the wall. With the abundance of fan mail, and requests for help she receives on a daily basis, I doubt that my letter made it past the mailroom! While blaming others provided a cover to hide under for a little while and an excuse to avoid dealing with my issues, it proved to be counterproductive. The power for change is always in the present moment; I wasted time sulking and giving away my power and responsibility to my situation.

*I also wasted my precious time punishing myself for being a "**College Dropout**" and worrying about what others would think or say about me. My depression clouded my mind, my decision-making, and my judgment. When you are depressed, angry, disappointed, and frustrated, you cannot focus on solutions or develop a new plan for your life. Getting unstuck is a conscious choice and your responsibility. No, you may not know exactly what to do or where to begin, but making the decision to create a new plan is an excellent start. Your intention to move forward will help you figure out what steps to take. Life may not always go as planned, so **If Plan A Fails, Don't Be Afraid To Execute Plan B!***

MY CHOICE:
**I choose to live life like riding a bus:
I am sensible and courageous enough to get off
and change directions if I find I am going the
wrong way, or I end up at the end of the line!**

SELF Talk

Is there an incomplete goal in your life that has you STUCK?

_____

_____

_____

Are you punishing yourself for making a wrong turn
or not accomplishing a goal?

_____

_____

_____

What current obstacle(s) can you turn into an opportunity
and/or work toward a solution?

_____

_____

_____

What past obstacle(s) have you overcome that you
can use as a future reference?

_____

_____

_____

SELF Talk

Which of your strengths helped you to scale that hurdle?

_____

_____

_____

_____

_____

YOUR CHOICE:

**You always have the power to make a new and
better choice to change your life.
Moving forward, declare your choice.**

_____

_____

_____

_____

_____

_____

Office Peon - *A person who does hard
or tedious work for very little money:
a person who is not very important in
a society or organization.*

Office Peon

Merriam-Webster defines a *peon* as a person who does hard or tedious work for very little money: a person who is not very important in a society or organization. Through additional research, I found that peon is a Spanish word for someone who has no control over their working conditions. When I started my first job, I wasn't exactly sure what a "*peon*" was or that I should be offended when it was used to describe me.

In the previous chapter, I spoke about my Stay-in-School job at Howard University. The Stay-in-School Program is a program offered by the government for students at area colleges and universities. It's very similar to a work-study position or an internship. A student works part-time while in school and full-time during vacation periods and the summer. I was excited about snagging a position because the job paid regular government salary rates. In other words, I was *ballin'*! And I was excited about working a *real* job.

My job title was "Office Automation Clerk". That sounds very official and important, right? Well, I thought so, and I couldn't wait to get started. I was working for the government of the United States. I had an official badge and had to walk through security every day. I might as well have been working directly in the White House alongside President Bill Clinton; that is how ecstatic I was at the time and how significant I felt. I did a variety of tasks at my new job: I answered phones, did the filing, sorted and distributed the incoming mail, delivered interoffice correspondence, and ordered and maintained office supplies. Some days I even had to catch the train over to the central office and pick up items. One of the best projects I worked on was helping to design new chairs for the office, from scratch. I like to think that somewhere in a government office in Washington, D.C. are chairs that I personally selected. I was learning so much and meeting some important people. On this job is where I met my first mentor. She was my very first supervisor, and she immediately took me under her wing.

One day I was told that I needed to attend a computer training workshop. The office was getting new software, and it was an executive decision that I would go to the training, learn what needed to be done and upload the software to every computer in the office. Then I was to take the computer software class and train the entire staff on how to use it. It was this brand new software called Microsoft Office.

I was reluctant to go. At that time, I didn't know anything about computers. A word processor was the latest and greatest gadget on the market. I didn't know anyone who had a personal computer. If I needed to use a computer, I had to go on campus to the computer lab. I shared with the receptionist that I didn't want to go to the training. They laughed and said that I didn't have a choice because everyone else in the office was too busy and that I was the "*Office Peon*." I chuckled a little because I did not know what that meant. I soon found out, and it changed how I viewed my role and position.

I attended several training sessions and learned more that I cared to about this new software. I remember mumbling under my breath that the training was probably useless because no one was ever going to use it anyway! Sorry Mr. Gates, it was my frustration talking! I was taking computer classes back-to-back and was getting tired of doing what no one else wanted to do. I complained to everyone that would listen. I even telephoned my grandfather back in Ohio to protest. He told me in his usual no-holds-barred way to suck it up and stop complaining. He told me that nothing I ever learned would be in vain. At the time, I rolled my eyes up in my head, sighed heavily, and hurried him off the phone. I continued having a private pity party because it was clear that everyone who I tried to invite to my party was not interested in attending.

Needless to say, every job I have had since my government job required me to use a computer and guess what else? You guessed it, Microsoft Office. I immediately became an office superstar because no one could work the new programs the way that I could. I knew how to use the many functions and shortcut keys. I knew how to maximize the programs to save time and energy and make work life easier. I would wow people when I built macros to automate functions. Sometimes I would show off by hitting one key and letting the computer do the rest. I had no idea that most people did not know how to use the many functions available in Microsoft Office. I assumed the intense training I received while working for the government was standard and required for all users. I took every class and every level of training available. I also trained the other staff, so I became a Microsoft Office pro.

Because of my training on installing software, I also learned how to troubleshoot computers when something went wrong. These expert computer skills enhanced my resume and helped me to land job after job, including my first graphic design position. I did not go to school for design. I am self-taught, and I learned most of my layout and desktop publishing skills working on newsletters and other creative projects while working for the government. I even served a stint as a layout designer for *The Hilltop*, Howard University's official newspaper. Over the years, I continued to hone these skills and eventually was offered the lead graphic design position at a major print shop. The owner was so impressed that I knew how to work all of the programs.

To this day, family and friends still call me to troubleshoot their computer problems and to help them navigate the latest software. I also do my own layout and design work. I designed the cover of this book you are reading and laid out the inside pages. I built my websites and created all of the logos and custom graphics. I love computers and gadgets, and they are a major part of my business. And just think, it all started with my exposure to computers and software while working as the "***Office Peon***."

LESSON
6

Nothing You Ever Learn Is In Vain!

*Many of us have been or maybe still are considered the "**Office Peon**." We have had to do things that we did not want to do. As a manager, I cannot tell you how many times I have heard an employee say or mumble under their breath, "That's not my job!" "That's not in my job description!" and my all-time favorite, "They don't pay me enough to do that!" Many people feel as if they are overqualified or too good to perform what they consider to be menial tasks, or tasks that are beneath them and their pay grade.*

Learning new things and volunteering to take on unwanted tasks can be a tremendous opportunity for you to grow, stretch, and expand your horizons. Because of my peon job, I learned to go above and beyond what is being asked of me. I have found that, not only do new skills enhance your resume, but they can make you an asset and a valuable human resource. In my last 9 to 5, I made myself a valuable resource. Despite my official job description, I learned everything I could about the company, answered the phones, assisted clients and customers when needed, performed graphic design, sold products, coordinated events, and volunteered for the projects that no one else wanted to do. This attitude and effort allowed me to work my way from a Senior Editor to Production Manager, to Creative Director, to my final position as Director of Operations and Creative Services.

Make it a habit to take advantage of every experience and

*opportunity that life has to offer. Be thankful for every opportunity you have to shine and to contribute your unique gifts, talents, skills, and abilities. When you are asked to pitch in and provide extra service, do it! Even when you are not asked, do it! Show everyone around you that you are a team player, flexible, versatile, and open to new opportunities. So what if you are not yet in your dream job or doing what you feel is your life's work. The Universe has a way of preparing each of us for the task and purpose that lies ahead. Being the "**Office Peon**" might be your stepping stone or the key that unlocks the position that God has for you. Even if taking on more responsibility and additional tasks do not immediately pay off, it will still enhance your skillset and prepare you for something new or a future opportunity. Everything you learn is valuable and can add worth to your life. Never be afraid to learn and expand your horizons because, like my grandfather said, "**Nothing You Ever Learn Is In Vain!**"*

MY CHOICE:
I choose to go the extra mile. I choose to take advantage of EVERY experience and learning opportunity!

SELF Talk

What task(s) do you despise doing?

_____

_____

_____

Do you feel you should be working on more important projects?

If so, what projects would you like to work on?

_____

_____

_____

What more can you do to contribute at work

or in your business?

_____

_____

_____

Do you feel you are where you are supposed to be

in your career (*at your job or in your business*)?

_____

_____

_____

SELF Talk

What is your next career move?

_____

_____

_____

What skills or knowledge have you acquired that can

help get you to this next level?

_____

_____

_____

YOUR CHOICE:

**You always have the power to make a new and
better choice to change your life.
Moving forward, declare your choice.**

_____

_____

_____

_____

_____

_____

Bankrupt - *A person judged by a court to be insolvent, whose property is taken and disposed of for the benefit of creditors.*

Bankrupt

I purchased my first car when I was 20 years old. It was a brand spanking new 1995 Ford Escort. It was all black and only had 11 miles on it. I was so proud that I was able to buy my car without a cosigner (remember, I was working for the government, and I was *ballin'*). Back then, I didn't know anything about credit, debt, annual percentage rates (APR) or financing. I merely handed over my credentials, let them run my credit, paid my down payment and signed on the dotted line. I was on my lunch break, and I caught the bus to the car dealership, not knowing that the process would take longer than my lunch hour. I went to one place; I didn't even think to shop around or look for the best deal. I assumed the sticker price told the entire and final story. I didn't care, I wanted a car! It's quite shameful now when I think back because I have no idea what I paid for that car. I knew the amount of my down payment and how much my monthly payments were, but I have no idea what my credit score was or how much that car loan cost me. In fact, I did not realize that my credit score was a factor in determining how much car I could afford; that it affected the amount required for the down payment and dictated the amount of my monthly car note. I didn't know anything about that relationship. And because I got the car on my own, without a cosigner, I didn't consult with anyone before I signed on the dotted line. After all, I was 20 and old enough to make my own decisions.

Growing up, I never learned about the importance of credit or credit scores. I did not have a bank account or any other type of savings until I started working for the government and needed an account for direct deposit. I take that back, I did have a few savings bonds that my grandfather had given me as a birthday gift, but all I knew about savings bonds is that they took forever to mean anything significant.

I saw my mother and grandparents work hard. I knew they paid bills, but I was never conscious of price or privy to how much anything cost. My grandparents owned a home and several cars over the years. My mother owned several cars as well. As for a home, we were renters. My mom rented numerous houses and apartments, and we moved around quite frequently. Over the course of my childhood, we lived in thirteen different apartments and houses. Because we moved so often, I did not learn the value and benefits of home ownership and acquiring assets. I never knew the exact reasons why we moved so much, and I never asked any questions. Honestly, I assumed that my mother bored easily and constantly needed a change of scenery. Although I did not have the benefits and stability of growing up in one neighborhood, moving around afforded me the opportunity to make many friends across the city. My mother did the best she could. She raised me and my sister alone and always kept a roof over our heads. Even though her parents worked and owned a home, my mother did not receive education in the home about finances, credit and money management. Her parents handled the finances, and she was not a part of their discussions about money. In turn, my sister and I were never taught lessons about finance in our home.

My first introduction to a credit card was in college. One day a credit card company was doing a promotion on the campus yard. I filled out an application and instantly was approved for my very first credit card right there on the spot. My first purchase was a Pear Glace lotion and body wash set from Victoria's Secret. A necessity I just had to have! I went on to splurge on many other items that I had been longing to have. I bought clothes for my daughter, an official Howard University starter jacket, a few pairs of new shoes, and a night out on the town complete with dinner at

Union Station. I was in credit heaven. That was until the first bill arrived.

I was shocked at the amount of money I managed to spend in such a short time. I had almost reached my limit. So, of course, I did the right thing; I paid the minimum balance due. I did not understand how to use a credit card. I thought it was simply another form of money to use when you didn't have the cash. I did not read the tiny details and fine print about finance charges, fees, and percentage rates. Again, I signed on the dotted line with no questions asked. I was getting pretty good at that. Not only was it a mistake to use a credit card on such frivolous and nonessential items, only paying only the minimum balance was not helping me either. By paying only the minimum balance, I bet it took me two years or more to pay off that starter jacket, and I can count on one hand how many times I even wore that jacket. In fact, some years later, I remember giving that jacket away, for FREE, to my cousin because it was taking up too much space in my closet.

You can imagine what happened once I got one credit card. B-I-N-G-O! I applied for more cards. I set a personal goal for myself to collect as many cards as possible. I was under the false impression that the more cards I had, the more credit I had. It was incredible that I could fill out a simple form and immediately get approved for a credit card and receive a colorful water bottle, book bag, T-shirt, or some other promotional tchotchke. Not to mention the hefty in-store discounts and special discount coupons I received for taking time out of my busy day to apply in the store. It was a magical process. It was even more excited when the cards arrived via mail. Yes, it was raining credit cards, and I didn't need an umbrella. The cards were beautiful and colorful and each one had my full name printed neatly across the front. It looked so official. I loved seeing my name on the cards, and it felt good to finally be in a position to get anything I wanted or needed (mostly what I wanted). It was too bad that the same people who approved credit cards weren't in charge of approving student loans and financial aid! I racked up credit cards from all of my favorite stores. I was very generous with my cards too, sharing them with friends in need and even buying things for my mother and my sister back home in Ohio.

Now keep in mind, I had several credit cards, a new car, and I still had never seen my credit score or credit report. By now I am sure you can see the writing on the wall. I was up to my eyeballs in something called debt, another unfamiliar term. I had a good-paying job and was spending all of my money paying bills. I didn't like feeling like I was working for free and knew that something had to give. So, I did what needed to be done, I stopped paying those darn credit card bills. I ignored their letters and phone calls and used my hard-earned money for more important and pressing matters.

Throughout my twenties, I continued to make reckless financial decisions. For instance, I traded in my first car for a larger car, with a higher monthly payment, right before my car was to be paid off for good. It makes no sense now, but back then I was trying real hard to prove that I was grown and capable of running my adult life. During this phase of my life is when I was actually *acting* like a *"Know-It-All."* I thought I knew everything, and that I didn't need to share anything with anyone. I didn't need anyone's approval and no one in my family knew I was deep in debt. On the outside, I was independent and had it going on. I had an apartment, a SUV, and a decent job, yet, I couldn't even answer my phone for all the bill collectors trying to track me down. And you would not believe how rude and ruthless some of those collectors were. The nerve of them, they acted like I personally owed them money!

When I was 24, my bad financial decisions came to a head. I was swirling in debt and working for free. Well, at least it felt like I was working for free because every bit of my paycheck was going toward bills. I barely had any money left after paying my monthly financial commitments. I was extremely unhappy and frustrated. I needed some relief. That's when I filed for bankruptcy. I had no clue what a bankruptcy was or the repercussions and the stigma often associated with filing. Someone told me that bankruptcy was a way to get rid of my outstanding debt and stop the rude and insensitive bill collectors from hounding me. That's all I really wanted. I needed a break, and I needed a fresh financial start. I had learned my lesson, and I vowed to never be careless with my finances again. Okay, so clearly it took way more than a pledge to get back on track. It took me well over seven years to repair my credit and bounce back from being "***Bankrupt***." I had to work hard at my finances and practice discipline. In fact, I'm still working hard and practicing every day to continue to make good financial decisions!

LESSON 7

Know Your Numbers!

Blaming and avoiding bill collectors and the institutions that trusted me with credit was insane. But as long as I made them out to be the enemy, I felt justified in not paying my bills. The bill collectors were doing their job, very well I might add, and I was only hurting myself and my credit by avoiding them and choosing not to pay on time. I was in over my head and was desperate for relief.

*It took me many years to get over being "**Bankrupt**" and to get back on track. I had to educate myself and to learn and understand the relationship between credit, APR, credit scores and credit reports. I learned that a credit score is very much like a GPA (terms I definitely understand). It is much easier to lower your credit score than it is to raise it. For this reason, you need to stay on top of your finances. The best way to do this is to know your numbers at all times. Know how much money you have in the bank. Identify and track how much money you have coming in and going out. And lastly, know where your money is going and what you are spending it on. I'm sure you can relate to how easy it is to break a twenty-dollar bill and then have no clue where the rest disappears to. You also need to stay on top of your credit. Get your free annual credit reports from the three main credit bureaus and monitor your credit score. There are several paid and free services that allow you to monitor your score and credit activity. You should know how much you are paying for credit and should,*

NEVER sign on the dotted line without having full disclosure of the agreement, payment terms, conditions, and penalties.

Paying bills on time is essential and managing money is a necessary skill. Have you ever tried to convince yourself that if you could get a raise, make more money, or win the lottery that you would become a better financial manager? I know firsthand what it feels like, no matter how much money you make, to still have to rob Peter to pay Paul. I know what it is like to live paycheck to paycheck, even when others might think that paycheck is pretty hefty. No matter your salary, how much money you make, or win in the lottery, if you are not a good money manager, you can still find yourself in a financial bind.

Education is key. Being educated helps you to better understand your options and gives you the ability to negotiate. Educate yourself about the credit process and how to make your money work for you and not against you. Establish a realistic budget that is within your means and accommodates your saving and investment goals. Do not spend more than you make.

*If you are a parent, please take the time to educate your children (before college if possible) about credit, budgeting, saving, spending, managing money, and the importance of paying bills on time. While parents do not have to fully divulge the family finances, it is wise to educate young people about the realities and responsibilities of managing money. We live in a day when most teens already have a debit card or access to a credit card without a solid education and understanding about how one swipe can change their lives. I am not anti-credit cards, I'm pro financial education. Whether you prefer cash, plastic or a combination of both, it is important to **Know Your Numbers!***

MY CHOICE:
I choose to be a GOOD steward
of my financial resources!

SELF Talk

Do you know how much money you currently
have in your checking/savings account(s)?

_____

_____

_____

How many checks have you bounced in
the last six months; in the last year?

_____

_____

_____

How much have you paid in overdraft fees or late fees in
the last six months; in the last year?

_____

_____

_____

How much money would you like to have in your
checking/savings account(s) by the end of this year?

_____

_____

_____

SELF Talk

When you make a major purchase, do you shop
around for the best price?

_____

_____

_____

Do you currently have a budget or a monthly plan to
track and manage your finances?

_____

_____

_____

YOUR CHOICE:

**You always have the power to make a new and
better choice to change your life.
Moving forward, declare your choice.**

_____

_____

_____

_____

_____

_____

HELLO
MY NAME IS

Married, Separated, Reunited, And Divorced

Married - *The state of being united to a person in a consensual and contractual relationship.*

Separated - *Estranged, parted, split up, broken up, living apart or separately.*

Reunited - *To come together again after a period of separation or disunity.*

Divorced - *Dissolution of a marriage.*

Married, Separated, Reunited, And Divorced

T his might be the longest chapter of the book, only because this is an area of my life where I have spent a lot of time and energy and have learned many lessons. I have to confess, here and now, I was never that little girl dreaming of Prince Charming and knights in shining armor. As a child, I never dreamed of or acted out my future wedding. In fact, up until I was in my early twenties, I never planned to get married. I was focused on being a good mother and having a successful career. Usually, the only time marriage came up was when I was feeling the heat from outside influences. Even though my parents separated when I was a young girl, I had other examples of long-time marriages and relationships in my life. My grandparents, who today have been married for over 50 years, were my primary example. My uncles and their wives were also examples. Still, my ultimate life plan did not include marriage. Imagine my surprise when I got bit by the marriage bug!

"*Married*" - They say that you find love when you are not looking. I'm not sure who *they* are, but I agree with them. And for me, that is exactly how it happened. It had been over a year since I ended a 6-year relationship and I wasn't looking for another one. I was refocused on completing my education and taking care of my family. I met my future husband at a church function, and we immediately hit it off. He lived out of state at the time, so our relationship began with long talks on the phone, which led to a long-distance courtship that culminated with a wedding proposal a year later. He proposed in the park one Saturday afternoon while he was in town. I was ecstatic to say the least and immediately said "Yes!" I felt ready to settle down. I now had two children (my first daughter mentioned earlier, and a second daughter from my six-year relationship). I wanted to provide them with a stable home. I also wanted a solid relationship and to build a strong family unit.

Despite my lack of planning and dreaming of being married as a little girl, my wedding day seemed to jump right off the pages of a storybook fairy tale. There were four ministers, a maid and matron of honor, five bridesmaids, two junior bridesmaids, matching groomsmen, a flower girl and ring bearer. There was a trumpet player and a harpist. The groom even surprised me with a serenade that had the entire church rocking from side-to-side and me blushing and grinning from ear-to-ear. At the end of the reception, a horse-drawn carriage rode us through the streets of downtown Columbus and delivered us to our honeymoon suite. The next day we were off to Disney World with the children in tow. A perfect start to a perfect marriage, and a perfect way to blend our new family.

Like most people, I never believed my marriage would end in divorce. I did not get married with the intention of getting divorced. I was sure that, after such a fabulous wedding and an outward display of our undying love and affection for one another, our marriage would last forever and a day. Unfortunately, two weeks after the honeymoon, I knew I had made the biggest mistake of my life! And even though I felt this way early on, I did not feel there was anything I could do to get out of the marriage. Could I change my mind? I felt like Private Benjamin after she enlisted in the army. *"Wait, I didn't know what I was getting myself into, I made a mistake!"* I felt like I had joined the armed forces, signed the official paperwork, and had already been sworn in to serve my country...FOREVER, until death do us part. In addition, I had moved out of state, gave up my apartment along with all of my personal furniture and belongings. I had given up my job and quit school once again in order to relocate. I had nothing and I could not imagine starting over from scratch. Where would I live? Would I be able to get any of my stuff back? On top of that, I had just had this elaborate wedding ceremony less than a month ago and received all of these expensive and beautiful gifts. We had spent so much money on the wedding and honeymoon. Not to mention the fact that my entire family and all of my friends were there to witness my commitment to forever. What would people think? What would my family say? How would my mother react? What would God think? After all, we were married in the church by four ministers. Oh yeah, and did I mention that my husband was the pastor of a church? This added another layer of confusion to the mix and was another reason I didn't feel I could end the marriage so quickly. Who wanted to disappoint and quit on God? Not me! I was 26 years old and trapped in what I thought was an impossible situation.

So, I did what many people do, I stayed in a bad marriage and tried to make the best it. I pretended that I was happy in hopes that one day I could truly be happy. I didn't want to fail at marriage, especially during the first few weeks. My grandparents had lasted for over 50 years, and here I couldn't even last a month. There was no way I could fail and face everyone. Besides, I had heard that the first two years of marriage were the hardest because two people have to learn how to live together and become one. Well, of course, when I heard that tidbit of advice, before getting married, I didn't think it applied to me. I was sure that my marriage was an exception to the rule and that my first two years of marriage would be nothing but pure bliss. I had also heard stories of arranged marriages where two people who barely knew each other were required to marry and build a life together. They learned to live together, and, over time, grew to genuinely love one another. If they could do it, so could I. Right?

Though my husband and I saw each other as often as possible during our long-distance relationship, I quickly learned that seeing each other once or twice a month is very different from living together in one space. I could not believe that my marriage was off to such a rocky start. What happened to the love I thought I felt?

What happened to the trumpet and the harp? My fairy tale was beginning to feel more like a nightmare. I couldn't understand, especially when I felt I had done everything right this time, and in the correct order. We had premarital counseling and did all of the things we were supposed to do leading up to marriage.

It turns out that my husband and I were inherently incompatible. Despite our counseling and the countless hours we spent talking and getting to know each other while we were dating, it was crystal clear after the wedding that we had different expectations about roles, responsibilities, family, love and marriage. I hear you thinking to yourself what I asked myself over and over again, If we were so incompatible, why did we get married in the first place? That is what bothered me the most. I was so sure that we were compatible. I thought we were on the same page and that we wanted the same things in marriage and life. I thought we had covered all of the bases in our premarital counseling sessions. Our pastor covered every ground. In my opinion, we couldn't have been more thorough than if we had met on eHarmony. com. Unfortunately, that wasn't the case and many of things we discussed in counseling never came to fruition in the actual marriage. There was also a ten-year age gap between my husband and I, which I think played a significant role in our relationship.

I spent many years being unhappy in my marriage and trying to *"make it work."* I used to put all of the blame on my husband because I felt his issues took center stage and appeared to be the main reason for our discord. In turn, I became angry and bitter. I was angry and bitter because I had given up so much to get married and it didn't turn out the way I had hoped. I had given up everything and relocated to a new city. I was angry with myself for, again, making a wrong decision. But mostly, I was furious with myself for continuing to stay and live in a home where I was not happy. I knew I deserved better, yet; I did nothing to change my situation. I felt justified in my anger because I wasn't getting what I needed in my marriage. I married for love and stability, and I wasn't getting either. I blamed my husband for our failing marriage. For years, I convinced myself that if he would change and be different, then I could change and be different, and then everything would be okay. The majority of my time and energy was spent trying to convince another human being to make the necessary amendments that I felt needed to be made in order for me to be happy. I can imagine now that my constant anger and pushing for change only fueled the fire and caused my husband just as much misery as I was experiencing. We were driving each other CRAZY, with both of us feeling trapped in a hopeless cycle. Through our many difficulties, we did manage to have a few fleeting moments of happiness and two additional children, but majority of the time we were masking what was really going on inside our home and our hearts. After eight years, we separated.

"*Separated*" - The years we spent separated were strange, joyous, and confusing all at the same time. I was on an emotional roller coaster. It was strange because our lives were in limbo. I wasn't physically living with my husband, but our public lives remained intertwined. We still attended the same church, worked together on several community projects and attended our children's events and activities as usual. Sometimes it felt like we were still operating as a married unit. But I have to be honest, the separation between our personal lives made me feel good! I liked being in my own space again. No, take that back, I LOVED being in my own space again. Finally, there was peace in my home and it physically brought me joy. I felt free. It was a confusing time because I wasn't sure if the separation meant I should move on with my life. For years, I had been searching for a way out, and now it was staring me in the face. It was also a very confusing time for our children who were being shuffled back and forth between two houses. They didn't fully understand what was going on and why they now had two of everything, one at mommy's house, and one at daddy's apartment.

"*Reunited*" - After two full years of separation, we decided to give the marriage one more try. The decision was based heavily upon the counsel of our pastor and advice from family and friends around us. Despite the fact that during the separation period, we didn't do anything to work on or change the marriage, we both agreed to give it another shot for the sake of our children. The one thing we did and still do have in common is that we love our children. We both wanted stability for our children and to provide them a home complete with a mother and a father, something neither of us had growing up. Looking back, we probably should have ended our marriage at that point. Getting back together did not solve our problems. Instead, it magnified the ongoing issues and exposed even more. Though we had a desire to raise our children with some normalcy, our situation was not normal. We immediately fell back into the same awkward and unhappy pattern.

During the two years we were separated, I changed. I was reintroduced to myself and regained my independence. And I liked who I was. I was no longer willing to live in an unhappy marriage, not even for the sake of my children. I found the courage and strength to leave for good. Yes, I regretted that I couldn't make my marriage work and provide the type of home that I wanted for my children, but I also realized that a mother and father without a loving relationship was not the example I wanted for my children.

"*Divorced*" - Marriage is one of those areas where you have to make decisions for yourself. No one can tell you when enough is enough or when it's time to give up and move on. Nor can anyone make you stay in a situation that isn't good for you. I ultimately had to take responsibility for marrying a man that I barely knew. We were incompatible. I was eager to be married and have the perfect family so I saw what I wanted to see. I spent too much time trying to change him and trying to make it work. It took courage for me to make the decision to leave for good. Finally, I did what was best for me.

78

LESSON 8

You Alone Are Responsible For Your Happiness, And You Can Only Change You!

It's often said that getting married is the easy part, but staying married is where the real work happens. I have a greater understanding of this now. Not only did I greatly underestimate the work involved in being married, but I had unrealistic expectations about love and marriage. I believed that if I loved my husband, that he would make me happy. I thought that by being married we would automatically have a strong bond and close relationship and that our family would be stable. I thought that by being married we would always be on the same page. And when two people are on the same page, they both get to read the book, right? Ha! I learned very quickly that not only were we on different pages; we were reading two very different books!

Aside from my erroneous assumptions, the biggest mistake I made in my first marriage was putting someone else in charge of my happiness. For the longest time, I blamed my ex-husband for not making me happy. I was also not completely honest about my real feelings, what I wanted, and what I needed from the relationship. Because I wasn't upfront about my needs, I made a lot of sacrifices that left me feeling unappreciated, unfulfilled, and disappointed.

Here's the NEWS FLASH...no other person (including your spouse), place or thing can "make" you happy. Happiness is a conscious choice. We often look outside ourselves for happiness, but happiness is a decision and a way of life. Regardless of what is going on around you, you can choose to be happy and you can also choose to make changes.

The second mistake I made was trying to convince someone else that they needed to change. You cannot make someone do something they do not want to do. The only person you can change is yourself. Authentic change can only take place when a person is aware of their faults, shortcomings, and limitations and are willing to take full responsibility for themselves and make changes. They have to want to change. In any relationship, if both parties involved are not willing to work on their individual issues, and then work together to fix and strengthen the relationship, that relationship will not work. It took me eleven years to realize this.

If you are in a relationship where you feel someone else needs to change, instead of being judgmental and attempting to fix the other person, begin making positive changes in your own life. Your change can positively influence those around you. When people see that you are making changes and improvements, they are often inspired (or convicted) to do the same. If your change does not better the relationship, it may be a sign that you need to change your relationship and your environment.

*Being **"Married, Separated, Reunited, And Divorced,"** taught me to take responsibility for my role in my relationships. These phases in my life also taught me to take responsibility for myself and not to play the victim. Whenever you blame others, you are not taking responsibility for yourself. You give away your power to create your own destiny and you remain a victim.*

In addition, I have learned that as human beings, we all bring our background and upbringing, our beliefs and values, and even our past issues and unresolved baggage into a relationship. These factors shape who we are, how we deal with others, and colors how we interpret our relationships. Within these few pages, I have shared my perspective. I cannot speak or write for my ex-husband as he experienced our relationship on his terms. If you ask him, he might have a very different perception and account of events. If you want to know his perspective, I guess you'll have to wait for him to write his biography or tell-all book. His issues, limitations, feelings, and thoughts are not mine to share.

Working on yourself, and dealing with your own issues is a full-time job! If your schedule is anything like mine, there are barely enough hours in the day to do the things that you need to do. You do not have time left in the day, or the energy, to try to fix or change someone else. After all, **You Alone Are Responsible For Your Happiness, And You Can Only Change You!**

MY CHOICE:
I am responsible for my happiness. I choose to be happy, not when, not after, but NOW! I also choose to be the change that I want to see in my relationships!

SELF Talk

Are you happy?

_____

_____

_____

You are happiest when…

_____

_____

_____

_____

_____

Is your happiness dependent on another person,
position, place or event?

_____

_____

_____

Are you overly critical or judgmental toward your
significant other, family members or friends?

_____

_____

_____

SELF Talk

Do you take responsibility for your role in your relationships?

_____

_____

_____

Do you often have advice, opinions and ideas for others on
how to better their lives and situations?

_____

_____

_____

Do you accept advice and feedback from others on ways
to better yourself, your life, and situations?

_____

_____

_____

YOUR CHOICE:

**You always have the power to make a new and
better choice to change your life.
Moving forward, declare your choice.**

_____

_____

_____

HELLO
MY NAME IS

Baby Mama

Baby Mama - *The mother of a man's biological child; especially: one who is not married to or in a long-term, intimate relationship with the child's father.*

Baby Mama

I have to be honest; this is one of the more complicated labels I have had to deal with and learn live beyond. While I was a teenage mother and a single parent, I was determined not to be perceived as the stereotypical "*Baby Mama*!" The moniker carries a very negative connotation, and no one wants to deal with a '*Baby Mama*" and all of her drama. You know the stereotypes, women who have children by multiple men, none of whom they are still with, and their lives are full of chaos. "*Baby Mamas*" are viewed as manipulative troublemakers who are bitter about their failed relationships and can't seem to let go of the past. "*Baby Mamas*" are seen as desperate, gold-digging, emotionally starved women who had a baby to either keep or trap a man. Then they use their children as pawns and as weapons of mass destruction, to dish out punishment and revenge. They wreak havoc in their exes' lives and interfere with new relationships. There have been numerous songs and books written about *Baby Mama Drama*, and we see countless exaggerated examples every day on talk shows, court TV, reality television, and even at the box office.

It is this depiction of a "*Baby Mama*" that gives so many undeserving young mothers and single mothers a bad reputation. Regardless of how hard some women try to manage their broken relationships, take care of and raise productive children, and live drama-free, they are still viewed as and considered to be *just* somebody's "*Baby Mama*." A position that is neither valued or respected.

Having had my first child while still in high school, my plan of only having children with the man I planned to spend the rest of my life with was severely derailed. I never intended to be anyone's "***Baby Mama***," or even a single mother, for that matter. I turned 17 a month after my daughter was born. Marriage was not an option, nor was a long-term relationship with my daughter's father. While I loved my daughter fiercely, I was young and had made a mistake.

Later, I dated my high-school prom date for five years after high school. During that time, we discussed getting married, but before we got serious about walking down the aisle, it became apparent that we were going in two different directions and wanted different things in our adult lives. I was working a full-time job and simultaneously working to complete my education. He was a musician and had dreams of becoming a rap star. When we mutually decided to call it quits, I found out that I was pregnant. I did not want to have another child with someone that I was not married to. Being that we were already on the verge of breaking up, I panicked. We decided to try again to save the relationship despite what we were both feeling inside. Yep, you guessed it; things still did not work out. A year after my second daughter was born, we broke up for good. I became a single mother of two. After my second daughter was born, I made a vow to myself that I would not, under any circumstances or conditions, have another child until I was married. Though I was able to keep that promise to myself, it did not change how some people viewed me or my situation. Nor did it change the personal guilt I sometimes felt for having two children without a solid family structure.

Because of this guilt, I found myself working overtime to set myself apart from the stereotypical "***Baby Mama***" and prove that I was, in fact, a good mother. During their early years, my daughters did not have much communication with their fathers. I avoided dealing with them at all. I voluntarily took on the responsibility of raising my girls alone. I convinced myself that this was the only way to avoid "the drama." I did not fight for child support or hold my daughters' fathers accountable for their responsibilities. I had made up in my mind that I did not want to be tied up in the court system or have to take off of work to make multiple court appearances. I didn't want to have to deal with mounds of paperwork and people poking around in my personal business, asking me intimate questions while all the while looking down at me and judging me for my decisions. Instead, I put all of my energy into my children and concentrated on being the best mother I could be. I put my girls in karate lessons, dance classes, and tried to ensure they had all of the benefits of a good upbringing. I kept a decent job and worked hard every day. I figured that if I was crowned "*Mother of the Year*," no one would notice that I was a young and single mother. And no one would think I was just someone's "***Baby Mama***."

When I got married, my husband did not have any children, and he was eager to start a family. He welcomed the fact that I already had children and that we were going to be an instant family. However; people around him were not so thrilled. Without even knowing the circumstances, I was judged because I already had children. There were people who did not feel that I was *good enough* for him, which again, caused me to question my own value and worth.

My husband and I went on to have two children together. When we started having problems in our marriage, I tried my best to work things out. Yes, I wanted my marriage to work, but even more so, I wanted a strong family unit for my children that included both a mother and a father. I did not want to get a divorce and be in a position where I was, yet again, a single parent raising not one, not two, but four children. While my life did not mirror the stereotypical "***Baby Mama***" images described earlier, I still shared their predicament. Even after getting married and trying to do things the *right* way, I now had four children and three different *Baby Daddies*.

LESSON 9

Your Current Situation, Condition, Or Predicament Does Not Define Who You Are!

Having four children from three different relationships, I spent many years feeling embarrassed and sometimes even ashamed to say that out loud. I always felt the need to explain just how my life took twists and turns, and how I ended up a single mother of four. I feared being judged. I feared that people would think I was promiscuous, not good enough, or worse, that I was somehow a bad mother. While I knew that I was not promiscuous and that I was a responsible mother, and that I loved all of my children and took care of them to the best of my ability, I struggled with self-worth. Was I good enough? Was I really a good mother? Did I make the right decisions when it came to caring for my children?

*The fathers of my first two children were young as well. But that did not release them from their responsibilities. Initially, neither of them held up their end of the bargain and I did not enforce it. I did not take the proper measures to ensure they fulfilled their responsibilities. I allowed my fear of being viewed as a vindictive "**Baby Mama**," to cause me to make erroneous decisions regarding my children's welfare. Their fathers deserved to be a part of their lives. My children deserved to be cared for and loved by both of their parents. And I deserved help and support raising my children.*

*Eventually, I got it right. I stopped making decisions based on the fear of being judged. I had to get clear about who I really was. I am not and have never been anyone's "**Baby Mama**."*

Yes, I made mistakes, but I was not my mistakes. My mistakes did not define who I was. Because I lost sight of my true worth and value and was ashamed of some of my decisions, I allowed others to make me feel bad about myself and make me feel like I wasn't good enough. I realize now that other people's thoughts and opinions would not have affected me if I had not been feeling a certain way about my own circumstances.

We all have said or done things we are not proud of. We all have secret parts of us that we don't share with anyone and, oftentimes, we define ourselves by these things. We must learn to have grace on ourselves and understand that we are so much more than our darkest, deepest regrets and failures. Your goal should be self-awareness, not self-scrutiny and judgment. Be kind to yourself. Celebrate your successes and wear your experiences proudly. Your past mistakes are meant to guide you, not define you. Be careful not to define yourself by your failures or your successes. While they each help shape you, they do not define you!

I am the proud mother of four beautiful, intelligent, and wonderful human beings. My children mean the world to me and I could not imagine my life without them. Regardless of the circumstances and how they came into the world, they are each special and have grown into amazing people.

At the time I am writing this book, my oldest daughter is 24. During high school, she was a stand-out athlete and received a track scholarship to a Division-1 college. After realizing her true passion, she switched gears and decided to become a personal trainer. She recently graduated and started her own business. My second daughter is in the military. She also ran track and participated in a special criminal justice program while in high school. She entered the service immediately after high school. My third daughter is a 4.0 student and a freshman in high school. Like her sisters, she too runs track. She has aspirations of being a fashion designer and makeup artist and owning her own company.

She told me that she wants to help make people happy, by making them look and feel good. My son, the youngest of the crew, is a little genius. He loves science and math and loves animals. He knows some of the craziest facts about animals and their habits. Sometimes I have to Google what he says because I am amazed that he knows such information. He plays football and loves the sport. When he grows up he wants to play in the NFL, be a veterinarian or a scientist, and then, after that, maybe become president of the United States.

*I am proud of my children and thankful for the privilege of being their mother. I am sharing this information to show that no matter where you come from, or where you are right now, **Your Current Situation, Condition, Or Predicament Does Not Define Who You Are!***

MY CHOICE:
I choose to recognize who I am!
I am not my mistakes!
I know my worth and true value!

SELF Talk

What mistake(s) have you made that you are
having a hard time getting over?

_____

_____

_____

_____

_____

What would be different in your life if you refused to
dwell on your past mistakes?

_____

_____

_____

_____

_____

_____

What lessons have you learned from your past mistakes?

_____

_____

_____

_____

_____

SELF Talk

Are there areas in your like that make you feel
guilty and/or ashamed?

_____

_____

_____

How do you usually deal with your guilt/shame?

_____

_____

_____

Do you love yourself? Why? (Explain your answer)

_____

_____

_____

_____

List the top five things you love and appreciate about yourself.

_____

_____

_____

_____

_____

SELF Talk

What are you still working on and learning to love

and appreciate about yourself?

YOUR CHOICE:

**You always have the power to make a new and
better choice to change your life.
Moving forward, declare your choice.**

HELLO
MY NAME IS

House Poor

House Poor - *A person who spends a large proportion of his or her total income on home ownership, including mortgage payments, property taxes, maintenance and utilities.*

Tamara Hartley

House Poor

I may not have made all of the right decisions or asked the right questions when it came to buying my first car, but I distinctly remembered the advantages and disadvantages of buying a new car versus a used one. While I was able to purchase a new car, I was not able to afford the bells and whistles and options that I would have liked. For instance, I could not afford the power window package. To open my windows, I had to crank the handle and manually roll down the windows on each side. Nor could I afford four doors, I had to settle for two and a hatchback. I could also only afford the basic radio package and sound system. Every time I asked about additional options, the price of the car went up, which meant my monthly payment would also increase. The alternative to buying a brand new car with limited options, was to purchase a used car that was fully loaded with options that I could not afford on my own. Options such as power windows, a sunroof, and a custom stereo with a 6-CD changer.

When it came time for my husband and me to purchase our first home, like buying a used car, I was sure that we could find an existing home with all the bells and whistles. However, my husband wanted to either build a house from scratch or purchase a property that needed rehabbed. We had some awful arguments about which direction to go with our new home, some that ended so badly that I didn't think we were going to make it into a new home. I eventually gave in and went along with the new build. I still was not convinced that it was the best route, but it sounded better and less dangerous than a property that needed to be gutted and rebuilt while we were living in it. And I was tired of arguing and living in a cramped two-bedroom apartment with three children and one on the way.

First, let me be clear, when you build a home from the ground up, you should be in a position to include everything you want in that home. I remember sitting in the sales office going over options and what we wanted in the home. I immediately had a flashback to sitting in that car dealership. Every option and upgrade came with a larger price tag. I was too nervous to add a door here or an extra option there because the bottom line number continued to grow. I was worried about the final price and the monthly mortgage payment. Naturally, I began to decline options and afterward felt like I didn't end up with the finished product that I really wanted. We poured most of our savings into the down payment and the few options we selected.

According to the lender who approved our loan, we could afford the house. We did not fudge any numbers or do anything inappropriate to get financing. But outside of paying our mortgage, we couldn't afford to do anything extra. For instance, I wanted a pool. I wanted to furnish every room and to finish the basement so that it looked exactly like the model home that lured us to buy the property in the first place. Unfortunately, those things were so far off into the future; that our children would probably be grown and out of the house before any of those things could be done. Our lives drastically changed, and we could no longer afford to live the kind of life we had grown accustomed to. We could not continue to do everyday things, like eating! OK, that is an extreme exaggeration, but it was clear that we had taken on more than we could handle and more than I was willing to work for or sacrifice. My husband was willing to work multiple jobs and willing to make cuts all around, I was not. I was not willing to sacrifice the time I spent with my family and their extracurricular activities. I did not want to have to work two and three jobs in order to make the mortgage. It seemed that after we paid the mortgage, we could not do much of anything else.

That was my first time buying a home, and, though I could clearly see the numbers when we were in the sales office, I went along with my husband. He owned other properties, and I ultimately felt he knew more about the benefits and the ins and outs of home ownership. I had also received counsel from a trusted church mother who urged me to follow my husband's lead. So, I did, despite the fact that my stomach was churning, and I felt uneasy about the final cost.

I admit, the house was beautiful; nevertheless, it was not my dream home. Yes, it was expensive and large, but it had little character and very little of me and my personal taste and style. I was unable to do the things I wanted to do in the house to make it feel like home because of the large monthly mortgage. Miraculously, we managed to live in the house several years. The first year was not that bad. We still had some savings and things were okay. I worked and contributed my portion to the house and our joint bills. I also worked a part-time job in the evening, but that was not meant to maintain the house. I worked this second job to pay for activities and extras for my children. They stayed involved in activities, and we traveled quite a bit.

I won't go so far to say that I was the kind of wife that didn't even know where the checkbook was. In fact, I knew exactly where it was, I simply chose not to deal with it. My husband maintained and paid the household bills, so once I contributed my designated portion, I did not have much more to do with the family budget. Based on the chronic headaches I often got when thinking about managing finances, I was more than willing to allow my husband to handle the responsibility.

Somehow, we fell behind on our mortgage payment and a few other monthly bills. We were able to recover because we were working extra jobs. Then it happened again and then again. Soon we were working two jobs each and the second job was no longer a luxury, but a necessity. We had to keep working to keep paying bills, which took the fun and relaxation out of my second gig.

I later learned that every time our mortgage payment fell too far behind, my husband renegotiated with the lender to get back on track, and the missed payments were added back into the balance which increased our monthly mortgage payment. Now I don't claim to be a financial wizard, but if you have trouble paying $100, why on earth would you now agree to pay $175? In essence, that is what was going on, and eventually our monthly mortgage was too much to handle. One afternoon, I was home alone and heard a knock at the front door. I could see a black and gold sheriff's car in the driveway through the sidelights on the door. *What on earth were the cops doing here?* I asked myself feeling a bit of panic. I quickly prayed that nothing was wrong with my husband or children. I opened the door to find a sheriff standing on the porch. He greeted me briefly and then handed me a large manila envelope. It was pretty thick and I had to grab it with both hands because it was heavier than I anticipated. I cautiously opened the envelope, and the contents immediately made my stomach turn. Court documents, our house was going into foreclosure.

I was confused and wanted to believe that this was some sort of a mistake or clerical error, even though, my gut instinct was telling me otherwise. I needed to talk with my husband. As I suspected, our mortgage had gotten out of control, and we were grossly behind on our payments. I was the last one to know because my husband did not want to worry me. Though I suspect the real reason he hid it from me was because he did not want to hear me say, "I told you so!" From the beginning, I had been against building the house because of the numbers. I felt it was too much for us to take on and still enjoy our lives. And it was evident that getting behind on a mortgage that size could be detrimental.

Things went downhill fast from there. Both of our cars were repossessed–another ambush via doorbell. I had no idea what was about to go down when I answered the door. I had a minivan at the time, and it was full of my children's things. I did not even have time to clean out the car. Luckily, the car company took the liberty of putting everything that I left in the van in large black trash bags and delivered them to our house. I felt violated as I sorted through the bags. The contents of the glove box, sports uniforms, sippy cups, spare change from the ashtray, and movies for the entertainment system were thrown in together. Many of the DVDs were cracked or split in two from the weight of the other content. It was a complete mess. Many of my items got ruined. I remember feeling embarrassed and angry at my husband for allowing this to happen. I was angry at myself for not going with my first mind and refusing to sign the papers for the house. I was also angry with myself for ignoring what was going on around me and not taking a bigger role and responsibility for our family finances.

Inevitably, we had to move and the stress of a foreclosure drove our family further apart. On top of that, the credit that we had worked so hard to build and maintain to secure funding for our new home was destroyed. I now had a foreclosure, repossession, and a tax lien associated with the property on my credit report. The light at the end of the tunnel was blown out by a massive thunderstorm.

LESSON 10

Live Within Your Means, And Never Spend More Than You Make!

Several years ago, I enrolled in a homebuyer's education workshop. I made myself a promise never to sign my name on another dotted line without fully understanding what I was signing up for. I wanted to learn the process of buying a home from start to finish. I wanted to learn the ins and outs of the purchase contract along with the terminology, acronyms, and the industry lingo. The workshop was a wonderful education. I learned about homeowner's insurance, the importance of a home inspection, property taxes, home equity, credit, closing costs, PPI (Payment Protection Insurance), and mortgage loans. It was truly one of the best decisions I have ever made for myself. Though all of the information was extremely helpful, the most beneficial thing I learned was about affordability ratios. These calculations help a potential buyer determine how much home they can afford, how much a lender will loan them, how much down payment is needed, and how much their monthly mortgage payment will be. The most important take-a-way being that just because a lender approves you for a particular amount, does not mean you have to buy a house for that full price. Instead, you should purchase a home based on the results of your affordability ratios that take into consideration your lifestyle and other financial obligations.

*I also learned through the workshop that my ex-husband and I were "**House Poor.**" We were working solely to pay for our mortgage and expenses and had little to nothing left after that.*

According to our affordability ratios, we needed to make almost three times our salaries to comfortably afford that house and to continue to live the kind of lifestyle we were accustomed to before we built the house. It became clear that neither the sales agent for the home builder or the realtor had our best interest in mind and the lender should have never allowed our deal to go through. We did not have the right people on our team. We later learned that several other families that worked with this same team eventually lost their homes as well. And while I am still convinced that we were victims of predatory lending, my ex-husband and I were ultimately responsible for signing on the dotted line and making the final decision to build a home that we could not properly maintain or afford. Even more so, I was responsible for going along with a plan that I knew in my heart wasn't the right fit or the right thing to do. I allowed my husband to bear the responsibility of our household and, by doing so, we both put our family and our credit at risk.

When you receive a raise, or get a better-paying job, it does not mean you have to go out and create bigger bills. That extra money can be used to invest in yourself, or to start your own business. It can also be used to start a savings account or an emergency fund. You do not have to spend it as fast as you make it. The bigger house, a fancier car, and designer clothes are fine and good if you can properly afford them, still maintain your quality of life, and still save and invest in your future. These items are accessories, not necessities. Nor do they accurately depict your reality or your level of success.

Purchasing a home is a significant investment and another example where education is critical. I do not blame my ex-husband for his desire for our family to live in a beautiful home in a prominent neighborhood, I wanted the same thing. However, I do wish we had taken a home buyer's class before we started house hunting. I wish we had searched out a better team to help us with the process. I also wish we would have opted for the used car with the bells and whistles!

I have been able to use my homebuyer's education in other areas of my life. Today, I am a better financial manager and pay closer attention to my credit and financial health. I take full responsibility for all of my financial decisions because I now understand that you should **Live Within Your Means, And Never Spend More Than You Make!**

MY CHOICE:
I choose to be fiscally responsible and to pay CLOSE attention to the details!

SELF Talk

On a scale of 1-10, with 10 being the highest, how would
you rate your financial health and why?

_____

_____

_____

Are you living within your means?

_____

_____

_____

Do you compare your financial life to others or have a
need to keep up with the Joneses?

_____

_____

_____

What money mistakes have you made?

_____

_____

_____

SELF Talk

What lessons have you learned from your money mistakes?

_____

_____

_____

YOUR CHOICE:

**You always have the power to make a new and
better choice to change your life.
Moving forward, declare your choice.**

_____

_____

_____

_____

_____

_____

Adult Learner - *A nontraditional
student, a returning adult student
who is usually 25 years and up who is
involved in forms of learning.*

Adult Learner

O ver the years I started and stopped several educational programs for various reasons. But finishing my education had always been a goal of mine. While this desire lay dormant, on and off, for many years, the desire never went away. So much in my life had changed since my days at Howard University. Though in college I had a child, worked a steady job and attended classes at the same time, my life had grown and my responsibilities expanded. I went from caring for one child to taking care of a family. I had more responsibilities and more people depending on me. Quitting my day job to go back to school full time was not an option. So naturally, I started exploring other options. I was surprised to learn that there were several colleges and universities offering nontraditional programs, meaning classes were offered at night, on the weekend, and even online through distance learning.

Like many people, I was skeptical of the nontraditional educational options. After attending a prestigious university, I was worried about program accreditation and if the world would accept my education or take my degree seriously. At the time, I was conditioned to believe that classroom education was the only option. After careful research, I concluded that entering a program designed for working adults was the best option for me and I am so glad that I did. Today, many institutions, including Howard University, have nontraditional educational options.

Through a mix of nontraditional options, I completed a bachelor's degree in business administration with a minor in marketing promotions. I went on to complete a dual-disciplined master's degree in marketing and communication. Getting back into the classroom was a challenge at first, and quite frankly, it required more discipline than my first time around. I enjoyed and appreciated the flexibility of my classes. Depending on my schedule, I took a combination of traditional classroom courses, accelerated courses, and online courses. I enjoyed online courses the best. They gave me the flexibility I needed to work full time and maintain my family-life balance.

Going back to school as an adult, I had a different focus and mindset. I was more focused on academics and future goals. I wasn't so concerned with joining clubs or hanging out on the yard. I studied hard and took every assignment seriously. It wasn't easy. Taking accelerated classes meant digesting a larger amount of material in a shorter period of time. That translates into multiple deadlines and a greater workload. Most of my assignments were research papers, PowerPoint presentations and group projects. Immediately after I graduated from the bachelor's program, I re-enrolled and completed the master's program. When I first got back into school, I felt like I was starting from the bottom. I felt like it would take eons for me to finish. But I stuck with it, and one day I looked up and it was my turn to walk across the stage and receive my degree.

Although each graduation is now a blur, I do remember the exhilaration I felt walking across the stage knowing that I had accomplished my long-standing goals. It also felt good to have my children by my side to witness my accomplishments. After all, they had taken the journey with me and endured my long nights of studying and group meetings. They were proud of me. And though everyone was instructed to hold their applause until the names of the entire graduating section had been announced, my children broke the rules and cheered loudly (despite the side eyes and daggers from other attendees) when the announcer called my name and I walked across the stage to receive my diploma.

LESSON 11

It's Never Too Late To Live Your Dreams And Accomplish Your Goals!

*I first entered college in August of 1992. I graduated with my bachelor's degree in May of 2007. I went in the college system as a traditional 18-year-old student fresh out of high school and finished as a nontraditional "**Adult Learner.**" It took me nearly 15 years to accomplish my goal. After many setbacks, starts and stops, and procrastination, I received my first academic degree from Franklin University in Columbus, Ohio.*

So often, we put our dreams, ideas, and goals on the shelf or the back burner because we are overwhelmed with work and overscheduled with activities and commitments. Like my father, we are often torn between what we have to do for others and what we really want or need to do for ourselves. Other people, priorities and responsibilities take precedence over our own needs and desires. At the end of the day, many of us do not have the time or energy to focus on what's for dinner, let alone time to focus on ourselves and accomplish our personal goals.

Our dreams can sit on the back burner so long that we convince ourselves that time is our enemy. We began to feel like time has somehow passed us by and that it is too late to follow our dreams. Other times we feel like we are playing Double Dutch, standing in one place, bobbing back and forth, waiting for the right time to make a move. Either way, we remain stuck and stagnant and often frustrated with our results.

I had a friend who tried to get me to start a degree program at the same time she started. I had every excuse in the book why "NOW" wasn't the right time. I had no idea where the money was going to come from; the kids were too young, I just started a new job. Because I seemed to have so many obstacles and lacked the motivation to find solutions to these obstacles, I convinced myself that it wasn't the right time for me to go back to school. I needed to wait until these issues were completely resolved or something changed. I needed to wait for the right time. Imagine my surprise three years later when I received my friend's graduation announcement in the mail. Wow, if I had started the program with her, I would have been done too! Instead of spending three years going to school, I spent three years just "thinking" about going back to school and making a move. I wasted time "waiting for the right time."

*While planning and preparation are a critical part of any process, they should not be used as an excuse to stand still and do nothing. If you are waiting for the perfect time to start living your life, you will be waiting FOREVER. There is no such time as the "right time." Life is full of twists and turns and there will always be challenges and hurdles in our way. Our job is to actively pursue solutions to scale these hurdles or simply move them put of the way. Our job is not to stand still and do nothing. Remember, there is no time like the present and time is not your enemy. **It's Never Too Late To Live Your Dreams And Accomplish Your Goals!***

MY CHOICE:
I choose to find balance, make moves and LIVE my dreams NOW!

SELF Talk

Are you living your dreams? If no, why not?

_____

_____

_____

What dream(s) or idea(s) have you put on the back burner?

_____

_____

_____

What do you feel you need in order to make your
dream(s) or idea(s) your reality?

_____

_____

_____

List the top five obstacles preventing you
from living your dream.

_____

_____

_____

_____

_____

SELF Talk

Now list at least one possible solution to each obstacle.

_____

_____

_____

_____

_____

_____

YOUR CHOICE:

**You always have the power to make a new and
better choice to change your life.
Moving forward, declare your choice.**

_____

_____

_____

_____

_____

_____

HELLO

MY NAME IS

Overachiever

Overachiever - One who performs, especially academically, above the potential indicated by tests of one's mental ability or aptitude. to perform better or achieve more than expected, especially by others.

Overachiever

W hen my youngest daughter returned to school after summer break to start her fifth-grade year, she found that many of her former classmates no longer went to the school. She asked her teacher, who told her that the students attended a special program for gifted and talented students at another building. My daughter immediately had questions because these were the students she had been in class with for quite some time and they were her academic counterparts. She knew that she performed at the same level as these students, if not better. She asked why she was not selected for the program as well. She then talked to the school principal and asked the same questions. Her inquiry turned into a meeting between the principal, the guidance counselor, her current teacher, her fourth-grade teacher and her parents. My daughter was not questioning if the other students should be in the program, she was questioning why she was not selected for the program when her grades, scores, and standardized test scores were always in the top percentile. She consistently made Honor Roll and often had the highest grades in the class. After going over my daughter's academic records, the principal agreed that the matter was something that needed to be reviewed. She asked my daughter if she was willing to go the long haul and take a series of tests to determine if she was eligible for the program. Of course, my daughter said "Yes!" That was a very proud moment for me. I was so proud of my 10-year-old daughter for recognizing her own talent and abilities, for having the courage to ask questions, and the boldness to stand up for herself. She was also willing to do what was necessary to follow through and make this opportunity happen. She was not the least bit deterred because she had to go through additional testing. And mind you, she had done this all on her own.

I had taken off work to attend the meeting. When I arrived, the guidance counselor met me at the door, shook my hand and said, "It is very nice to finally meet you. Your husband told me that I was going to have to watch out for you today because you are one of those "**Overachiever**" types, and your daughter takes after you." The comment initially took me off guard. This meeting was my first encounter with the counselor. *What did she mean by "***Overachiever***" type?* Was she implying that my daughter's efforts were not genuine or warranted? Or maybe that I was an obnoxious, pushy parent trying to get my daughter into the gifted and talented program by any means necessary? Or maybe she feared I was going to be defensive or upset and come into the meeting with my earrings off and a jar a Vaseline ready to raise hell or start a fight. I was none of the above. In fact, I was not there to plead my daughter's case. She had already done that herself, and very well I might add. As her mother, I was there to support her efforts. Getting into this program was important to her, so it became important to me. I also agreed that if academics were the sole criteria, based on her track record, my daughter should have been included in the program. I was there to learn more about the program and the selection process. I was willing to allow my daughter to go through the process and wanted to show her that she had my full support and that I did indeed have her back. As a mother of four, my children cover the academic gamut. While I have always maintained a high standard of excellence and commanded that all of my children do their very best, some of them struggled academically more than others. I'm only sharing that information to show that I am just as supportive of all my children and did my best to provide tutors and whatever academic resources were needed. I have never tried to unjustly bogard their way into a program simply for my own bragging rights or to feed my own ego.

I looked the counselor dead in the eye, making sure to show a look of confusion on my face, when I asked, "***Overachiever***? What does that mean? Certainly, it can't mean that I achieve too much so I'm assuming it means that I strive for excellence and do my best at all times. And if that's the case, I think everyone should strive to be an ***Overachiever,*** don't you?" The counselor was speechless and stared blankly at me. I smiled sweetly, walked away and took a seat. Now I was on the defensive. And I was even more upset that my husband had initiated that comment. I made a mental note to deal with him later. I wasn't sure what was about to take place in the meeting, but I was not going to let anyone, not even her own father, belittle my daughter's efforts or discourage her from pursuing the gifted and talented program. Nor was I about to let my daughter get denied an opportunity simply because, like her mother, she was perceived as being an "***Overachiever***."

After several rounds of testing over a two-day period, my daughter did not get into the program. Though she scored very well on the tests, she was three points shy of making the cut. As it was explained to us, because of the funding and strict guidelines of the program, the district could not bend the rules and allow her in based on her final composite score. As you are thinking right now, I too thought that they should have made an exception based on my daughter's track record and her effort and cooperation with the process. This decision could have been a setback to my daughter's educational process or her emotional well-being. She could have felt that she had somehow been wronged or targeted and that the system was rigged and unfair. She could have acted out or rebelled against her teachers. But her attitude and how she handled the news taught the adults in the room yet another lesson.

My daughter shrugged her shoulders and quickly shook off any disappointment. She told us that she had done her very best on the testing, which is all she could do. She was happy with her performance because she knew that she had done her best. And she thanked everyone in the room for the opportunity to try.

The administrators were impressed with my daughter's reaction and gratitude. They each encouraged my daughter not to worry too much about the testing process; after all, she was still a full year younger than the other fifth grade students in her class and the students in the gifted program. My daughter did relish for a while in the fact that, as the youngest student in the entire fifth-grade class, she had scored so well on the tests. She then immediately turned her focus to the sixth grade. She made up her mind that day to get straight As that year to ensure that she would get placed into the gifted and talented program in middle school.

LESSON

12

Strive For Excellence!

*That meeting with the guidance counselor was not the first time I was referred to as an "**Overachiever**," and quite frankly I still do not understand why the word is often used in a negative way. According to Merriam-Webster, an overachiever is one who achieves success over and above the standard or expected level especially at an early age. When did it become a negative thing to achieve success or to go above and beyond? The alternative to striving for excellence and doing your best is settling for mediocrity or being average. Settling is a choice, and because one person is comfortable being average does not give them the right to ridicule another person for striving to be excellent.*

*Another time, I was told that the reason I was as an "**Overachiever**" was because I was overcompensating for some area of lack in my life. That I was trying to get the approval, attention, and validation that I unconsciously craved. So, let me get this straight, the reason I achieve and attempt to do my best is because I lack in another area of my life? While I believe in psychology and I recognize that there are proven commonalities in human behavior, I do not believe that everyone can be diagnosed the same or put into a box. Long before my parents split up, I was striving for excellence. It is who I am, part of my DNA. I refuse to believe otherwise or allow myself to give a temporary circumstance or life experience credit for my hard work ethic and dedication to excellence.*

There are times when people try to make their issues your issues. What they do not see for themselves, they definitely do not see for you. Then they attempt you make you feel bad because you chose not to settle and decided to follow your dreams. You chose to go back to school to finish your degree. You made the decision to work hard and stay overtime to get that promotion. You chose to save and invest your money rather than splurge on a latest handbag or designer label. People often want what you have and want to be where you are, but they are not willing to make the same choices and sacrifices you have made in your life to get where you are.

My youngest daughter is one of the most self-confident people I know. She is very clear and unapologetic about who she is. I remember at her kindergarten graduation, she was asked what she wanted to be when she grew up. At four years old, she spoke clearly into the microphone, "An artist, like I already am!"

Sometimes a strong display of self-confidence is viewed by others as a form of narcissism or conceit. Self-confidence can be intimidating to others, particularly those who do not have as much belief or confidence in themselves. You may be made to feel bad because you are self-confident. I encourage you to continue believing in yourself no matter what. Let others know that your shine has nothing to do with them, but everything to do with you and your commitment to always be the best you that you can be. You are like the sun and have no choice but to shine. If others can't stand your shine, buy them a pair of sunglasses!

There is no need for competition, jealousy, or comparison. We all have different gifts and talents, and different goals in life. God has a specific plan for each and every one of us and has placed different desires in our hearts. The Universe is abundant, and there is enough success and prosperity to go around. Though everyone may not have access to the same resources, everyone has the power of choice. Do not allow others to make you feel guilty because you have a dream, have made different choices in your life, and have achieved a level of success. Do not allow others to make you feel guilty for wanting more or something different. Continue to go after your dreams and **Strive For Excellence** *in everything that you do!*

MY CHOICE:
I choose to be like the sun and
SHINE no matter what!

SELF Talk

What you believe about yourself defines who you are.

What do *you* believe about *you?* Who are you?

_____

_____

_____

Are you assertive? Do you speak up for yourself?

_____

_____

_____

In what area of your life have you been burying

your voice and not speaking up for yourself?

_____

_____

_____

Are you willing to go the extra mile to get

what you want and deserve?

_____

_____

_____

SELF Talk

What are your personal standards?

_____

_____

_____

Do you strive for excellence and always

seek to do your best?

_____

_____

_____

YOUR CHOICE:

**You always have the power to make a new and
better choice to change your life.
Moving forward, declare your choice.**

_____

_____

_____

_____

_____

_____

Remarried - A person that marries again after they have obtained a divorce from their previous husband or wife, or after their previous husband or wife has died.

Remarried

B ecause I spent so many years feeling unfulfilled in my first marriage, when it was clear that it was over for good, I was relieved. Not relieved that the marriage didn't last, but relieved that a painful period in my life was over. I felt like I had been given another chance, another opportunity for happiness. My family and friends built a wall of protection and support around me. A group of my close friends even threw me a divorce party to cheer me up and to make sure that I was okay. I remember showing up at the venue and the maître d' asked if I was there for the "Divorce Party." I was tickled by that phrase and at how serious she was when she asked the question. I smiled and answered "Yes, I guess I'm the guest of honor."

Starting from scratch and picking up the pieces from a broken relationship isn't easy and I had to make quite a few adjustments as I moved back into my own house and started over, again. I was in a pretty good place mentally and emotionally. Though my marriage had ended, I was not bitter. I had not given up on love and knew that eventually, in time, I would be able to move on. I was not looking for a new relationship. I threw myself into my work and my children. I was traveling quite a bit and keeping myself busy. About six months after I had moved out, I received an unexpected message through Facebook from an old friend and classmate. He was inquiring about our 20-year high school class reunion. I was the senior class president, and he was vice president, so it was our joint responsibility to get together and coordinate a reunion. Aside from our senior offices, we were also very close friends from the moment we met freshman year. And it wasn't a secret that he wanted to us be more than just friends.

He would often tell me and others that I was his "*Dream Girl*." I liked him too. At one point around graduation we discussed giving it a go and possibly attending the same college, but it didn't work out for us that way. He received a football scholarship to Bowling Green State University and I had my heart set on Howard. We parted ways. We stayed in touch sporadically throughout college, and eventually lost touch as our lives took us in two different directions. I've thought of him often over the years and even Googled him a time or two to see what he was up to. Though I never verbalized it, to me, he represented "the one who got away." I often wondered what would have happened if we had attended the same college. What would our lives have been like?

His initial message was simple. "Hey, how are you? What's going on with the reunion? We should get together and discuss." He left me his number. I was traveling to Atlanta, Georgia, that day and quickly replied to his message with my number and said "Let's talk." A few weeks went by before I heard from him again. This time he sent a text message. I was again traveling, headed to St. Louis, Missouri for an event and a planned pit stop at the infamous Sweetie Pie's soul food restaurant for some of Mrs. Robbie's famous macaroni and cheese. I was boarding the plane and I quickly texted back. "I'm heading out of town, let's get married when I get back." *OMG! What was I thinking?* As soon as I hit the send button, I couldn't believe I had just done that. As I was shaking my head in disbelief, he texted right back and said, "You were always supposed to be MY wife!"

When I returned home, we agreed to get together for dinner and discuss the reunion. Needless to say, we met for dinner and never parted ways. We fell right back into our familiar friendship as if 20 years hadn't passed. Though the planning fell through, and we did not have our high school class reunion, we had our own reunion.

Again, I was not looking for a new relationship, and I certainly wasn't looking to get "***Remarried***." The ink was barely dry on my divorce papers! I was not trying to rush back into marriage. I became nervous about the relationship and began to feel like it was too good to be true. Did I really deserve to be this happy? I was looking for reasons to back out and trying to talk myself out of it, and almost did. I almost called everything off because it felt too good and unbelievable. I was happy, truly happy. Everyone saw a change in me, including my children. This man had come back into my life and showed me the meaning of unconditional love. This was the type of storyline Shonda Rhimes reserved for her television plots or something you witnessed only on the big screen. This didn't happen in real life, especially not in my life. I had witnessed first-hand how fairy tales could quickly turn into nightmares. I absolutely wasn't excited about starring in that role again.

A year and a half after I proposed via text before getting on an airplane, we were married. This time around there was no trumpet, no harp, no huge wedding party or horse-drawn carriage. It was a simple ceremony downtown with just the two of us and the minister present. It wasn't fancy, and still it was more special than any wedding I could have ever planned. I had been given a second chance. A second chance at love, a second chance at happiness, and a second chance with the one who got away.

Everyone Deserves A Second Chance, Even You!

*I almost missed another chance for happiness. At first I told myself that I didn't want to get married because I was afraid of what people would think about me being "**Remarried**" so soon after getting divorced. After digging deeper, I realized that was not the reason. While I cared about the opinions of my children and family, I have never been one to let other people stop me from doing what I wanted to do. I knew it was more than people's negative talk that had me apprehensive. The truth was, I was still blaming myself for my failed marriage, and I didn't think I deserved to be happy.*

One of my favorite authors is Louise Hay. In her book, You Can Heal Your Life, she states that "If we deny our good in any way, it is an act of not loving ourselves." I was not only "not loving myself," but I was also "punishing myself" because I didn't feel worthy of happiness. Sometimes we sabotage our happiness because we have convinced ourselves that, for whatever reason, we do not deserve it. We blame ourselves for past decisions, actions, mistakes, and the role we might have played in a bad situation. Others can forgive us, and we can forgive others, yet we have a hard time forgiving ourselves which can block goodness from coming our way.

Imagine right now that you are on the telephone with your best friend or your child. They are crying uncontrollably and upset over a huge mistake they have made. The mistake is a costly one, and one they wish they could take back, but they can't. The mistake has an adverse effect on their lives and those around them, possibly even you. What do you say to your best friend or your child at a critical moment like this? Most likely you will begin to try and comfort them. Tell them that everything is going to be okay and that they will get through this. You may even begin to help them brainstorm possible solutions to the problem. You tell them that you love them and that you will do whatever you can to help them through this difficult time. You are loving, kind and compassionate because you truly love them, care about their well-being, and want nothing but the best for them. Even when they are dead wrong, you can still manage to muster up some support and empathy.

Now imagine the same scenario only this time it is YOU who has made a terrible mistake that adversely affects you and the people you love. What do you say to yourself? I am going to go out on a limb and say that your self-talk will be vastly different and may sound a little like this. "You are so stupid!" "How could you be so stupid?" You know better than this!" "You are better than this!" "You had no business doing that!" "You are an idiot!" "I HATE you!"

Does this sound familiar? Even if you don't go this far, you are still most likely to be harder on yourself than you would be with your best friend or your child. Why is it that we are so nurturing and encouraging to other people, and so negative and hard on ourselves, especially when we make a mistake? We punish ourselves and don't give ourselves the same grace.

We have to get to the point where we are our own best friend. We have to love ourselves and learn to forgive ourselves when we make mistakes or wrong decisions. This includes allowing ourselves to be happy and welcoming good into our lives. You wouldn't hold a grudge against your best friend or your child, not for long at least. So why hold a grudge against yourself? You should love you more than anyone else loves you. Loving yourself is essential and opens you up to the good that life has to offer. It is true that if you do not love yourself, you will never truly be able to love anyone else or experience unconditional love.

What do you need to forgive yourself for? Do you have an area in your life where you are holding yourself hostage and keeping yourself from experiencing happiness? What will it take for you to set yourself free? Are you willing to give yourself a second chance at happiness? Do you deserve a second chance at happiness? In case you missed it, the right answer to that question is YES! **Everyone Deserves A Second Chance, Even You!**

MY CHOICE:
I forgive myself and I am my best friend.
I deserve to be happy. I choose to allow happiness into
my life and RECEIVE all of the goodness
that God has planned for me!

SELF Talk

What do you want in your life that you do not currently have?

_____

_____

_____

Do you feel you deserve what it is you
are wanting in your life?

_____

_____

_____

Do you take responsibility for your mistakes?

_____

_____

_____

How do you handle making a mistake?

_____

_____

_____

Are you your own best friend?

_____

_____

_____

SELF Talk

Do you easily and quickly forgive yourself?

_____

_____

_____

Are you holding anything against yourself?

If so, what and why?

_____

_____

_____

YOUR CHOICE:

You always have the power to make a new and better choice to change your life. Moving forward, declare your choice.

_____

_____

_____

_____

_____

_____

Control Freak - *A person who feels an obsessive need to exercise control over themselves and others and to take command of any situation.*

Control Freak

O ne day, while I was folding a load of laundry, it hit me like a ton of bricks and I had an Oprah "aha moment" (*Yes, of course I started watching Oprah again - ha!*), I was a "***Control Freak***." I was tired from working a 12-hour day. I came home, cooked dinner, and was up to my eyeballs in household chores. I was tired and really wanted to lay down, but there was too much work left to be done. I thought about asking my children to help, but quickly changed my mind when I remembered that they never folded my towels correctly. Nor did they know how to properly fold T-shirts and underwear into perfect squares and triangles. If I let them help, I would just have to go back behind them and do it again, the right way. I finished folding the clothes and called on each child to come get their pile and put their clothes away. Later that evening, I went into my son's room to put some additional items away and I was appalled to discover that he had haphazardly thrown the clothes and underwear, that I have just meticulously folded, into his drawer. I then checked my daughter's rooms and found the same thing. No one cared that I had just spent my precious time, as exhausted as I was, folding each piece of clothing or how perfect my folding was. There I was stressing and overworking myself only to find out that I was the only who cared about perfectly folded underwear. The next load of laundry that came out of the dryer, I dumped the basket over onto the floor and had each of them fold their own clothes.

I let go of a lot more than a basket of laundry that night! I realized that my need to have laundry folded a particular way was rooted in my need to have complete control. I was refusing to give up my personal control, even if it meant doing the job all by myself. Even the occasional times in the past when I did allow the kids to help me fold, I completely dictated the process, so much so, that we all left the experience frustrated.

Throughout my life I have been accused of being a "***Control Freak***" by my spouse, my children, other family members, and even some of my coworkers and employees (though in the workplace it is affectionately, or not-so-affectionately, called a micromanager).

I was initially in denial of this label because I didn't see what I considered to be love and a constant strive for excellence as being a "***Control Freak***." I felt that by taking a personal stake and actively participating in affairs and matters that personally concerned me, my job and business, or affected the ones I loved, that I was being responsible, supportive, managing expectations, and getting the J-O-B done! I had a self-proclaimed "S" sewn on my chest because I was always multitasking, putting out fires, and working around the clock. If I saw a potential problem or catastrophe waiting to happen, I stepped in to save the day. And sometimes, to avoid having to step in later in the process, I would simply handle the task, job or situation myself from the get go. Then after working myself to the bone, I would feel drained and exhausted. I would run out of gas and wonder where my help was. This became a pattern in my personal and professional life. I would work long hours, take on too many tasks, and, before long, feel overworked and underappreciated. Then I would complain that there was no rest or help for the weary.

I didn't set out to be a "***Control Freak.***" I wasn't trying to control or manipulate others. I realized that my need to dictate everything around me was not about wanting additional control, but rather about not giving up my *personal control*. I also had a hard time trusting others. Not because they were untrustworthy, but because I had a hard time trusting others to do their part, to take responsibility, and to care about the results and outcomes just as much as I did.

When I went back to school, I was surprised to see that teaming and group work had become a big part of the learning process. I had been used to doing my own work and earning my own grade. In group learning, every member of the group shares responsibility for the outcome. In the beginning, I had a hard time with this. I would completely take over a project because I did not trust the work ethic of the other group members. But over time, I learned how to become a team player and how to share the responsibility. I learned that everyone has a level of skill and unique contributions. I was not the only person striving for excellence. I eventually became appreciative of the support system that developed from working in a group.

Management was another great training ground for me. As a manager, I learned how to delegate without dictating. By hiring talented and capable individuals, I was able to delegate and not take on too many tasks. This allowed me to lead the team and focus on other responsibilities. I began trusting my staff to do their part and empowering them to take ownership of their work. By doing this, I quickly learned that they cared about the results just as much as I did.

I have always been independent. And over the years, especially during my years as a single parent, I learned how to rely on myself. I had to do things and figure things out by myself. In other words, I became used to doing things "*my way*." And just like with the laundry, I had to learn how to trust others in other areas of my life and learn how to rely on others to share the load (no pun intended)!

We All Need Help Sometimes!

Just like me, many of you were raised to be strong, independent, and very PROUD. We grasp how to give help, but have trouble receiving help from others. How many times have you ignored a friend or family member's request to "Let me know if there is anything I can do." or "Let me know if you need help with that." We often nod our heads and politely say, "Thank you!" with no real intention of taking that person up on their offer. We fear being too vulnerable and opening ourselves up to others.

Review the following scenarios to see if you can relate:

1) You subconsciously feel that asking others for help is a sign of weakness or that asking for help somehow makes others believe that you are not self-sufficient or that you don't have it all together. In the end, you end up stressing yourself out or stretching yourself too thin trying to do too much at one time and on your own.

2) You confuse strength with perfection. You keep up a strong front because you do not want others to know that you messed up or got yourself into a jam. You have a need for others to think you are strong and perfect. Newsflash...NO ONE is perfect, not even you! We all make mistakes.

3)   You have control issues. If you cannot control people or situations, you avoid dealing with them all together. You do not have faith in other people's capabilities to properly handle the details and to do the right thing. On your job or in your business, you have a hard time delegating to others and allowing others to help because you are unsure of their abilities to perform. You believe that if you do not personally handle a task or oversee it (micromanager 101), it will not get done correctly. You are part of the group that invented the saying, "Want something done right, you have to do it yourself!" Even when you have made it a point to surround yourself with quality and capable people, you have a hard time relinquishing control and allowing them to play their part. As a result, you take on too many tasks and projects, which opens the door to unnecessary stress in your life.

At some point in my personal life and career I can say that I have operated in each of the above scenarios. There were many times in my life when I needed help. Sometimes I asked for what I needed, but more often than not, I tried to handle everything on my own. I am an independent woman and have been managing my own affairs for a very long time. There was something in me that refused to ask for help. Call it pride, ego, or plain stubbornness. Whatever the case, I was more comfortable relying on the team of me. Asking others for help meant bringing someone else into my personal space and me having to explain myself, my actions, and decisions. It was easier to work things out on my own.

By not asking for help, you are not only putting pressure and stress on yourself, but also on those who care about you. Your family, friends, mentors, and other members of your support team care about your well-being and want nothing more than to see you happy, healthy, and prosperous. Not allowing the people who love you to help you is selfish. We were not put on this great earth to live alone or operate in isolation. We are designed to live in community and to help one another.

Asking for help is not a sign of weakness. Trusting others and allowing them to hold up their end of the bargain, relationship, or agreement is not a sign of defeat. As a young parent and college student, I wanted to prove that I could be on my own and handle my business. I have since learned that being an adult is not about handling everything on your own, or having all of the answers. Part of being a grownup is being wise enough to discern when, who, and how to ask for help because **We All Need Help Sometimes**!

MY CHOICE:
I understand that I do not have to carry the load alone. I choose to be honest about what I need and ask for help when needed. I do not always have to be in control, and I CAN trust others.

SELF Talk

What situations or areas in your life do you
need to let go of control?

_____

_____

_____

Is it difficult for you to ask for and accept help from others?

_____

_____

_____

Name at least five people who you trust and
can lean on for support.

_____

_____

_____

_____

_____

Do you trust others to perform and fulfill their
end of an agreement/relationship?

_____

_____

_____

SELF Talk

What area(s) of your life/work could you use some

additional help, assistance or resources?

_____

_____

_____

YOUR CHOICE:

**You always have the power to make a new and
better choice to change your life.
Moving forward, declare your choice.**

_____

_____

_____

_____

_____

_____

Jack Of All Trades, Master Of None
- *A person that is competent with many skills, but spends too much time learning each new skill that he/ she cannot become a master in any particular one.*

Jack Of All Trades, Master Of None

W hen I was a child; I was fascinated with Diana Ross. At a young age, she was the only person I knew who commanded people's attention from the stage. I had seen her in The Wiz and watched her televised concert. She was beautiful, graceful and changed her clothes every few minutes. People loved her, I loved her, and she exuded so much energy and charisma through her music. I wanted to be like Diana Ross. I later learned that I did not have her vocal abilities, but I did share her love for being on stage and mesmerizing a crowd. I too had stage presence, and I loved doing anything that allowed me to be in front of people. Whether it was starring as Maria in the kindergarten production of *The Sound of Music,* or reciting a poem for the annual oratory contest. Throughout middle school and high school, I was always involved in leadership and special projects. I loved presenting my science fair and history day projects and consistently advanced to state and regional competitions. I ran for student council, class office, and homecoming queen and had to give speeches in front of the entire student body. I felt natural on the stage, yet when it was time for me to go to college, I did not select a career path that would allow me to use my natural gifts and talents.

While I gravitated to being on stage, giving speeches, and connecting with people, I did not know how to turn that into a career other than becoming a politician and I could not see myself in a political career. When I entered college, I was a chemistry major. After being encouraged to select a career and profession that would make money and ensure I would always have a job, I thought I would become a neurosurgeon. When I think about that now, it makes me laugh. Could I have been a doctor, of course I could have been if that's what I set my mind to. I took advance placement chemistry in high school and my teacher encouraged me to major in chemistry. At 18, it sounded impossible to choose one profession to work in for the rest of my life. It seemed so limited and confined. What if I didn't like the profession I chose? Would I have to go back to school to learn a new one? The pressure was overbearing.

As I entered the workforce full time, I still had no idea what I wanted to do with the rest of my life and had yet to make a connection with something I truly enjoyed doing. I took jobs to take care of my family and responsibilities, not because they fulfilled an innate desire. Because I have always been a creative soul and full of ideas, I began seeking out positions in the creative realm. I held positions in the areas of branding, marketing, communications, writing, editing, graphic design, and public relations. No exaggeration, I have worked in all of these areas. One of the downfalls of being multitalented is that it can become hard to focus on or find the one thing that brings you the most passion and joy. It was hard for me to keep still and focus on one thing. I was becoming a "***Jack Of All Trades***," but still unable to pick the one area I wanted to master. I was not content doing repetitive tasks all day long or completing tasks that required little to no creativity. I would land a new job and quickly become bored. Get another job and, just as quickly, become bored and dissatisfied. I seemed to switch employers or positions every three years.

There was a point in my life where I thought I wanted to become an actress. I thought it would satisfy my desire to be on stage. I seriously contemplated packing my bags and moving to Los Angeles. But because I was a mother with small children, I did not think it was wise to uproot my family and travel across the country. I was afraid of being a "starving artist." As an alternative and a creative outlet, I started doing voiceovers and commercial work on the side. I took acting classes and found a local agent.

I immediately began to book jobs and even landed a regional commercial. Though this was not my full-time gig, being in front of the camera revived my love for being on stage and I liked seeing myself on television. While I enjoy acting and still do work today, I realized that it was not my ultimate purpose or calling.

I finally found a job that seemed to suit me better than all the others. In this new job, creativity and multitasking were requirements. I was able to be creative and use my degrees and skillsets. I was afforded the opportunity to travel the country and meet and network with some of our nation's best and brightest stars; many of whom are well-known celebrities, politicians, corporate CEOs, executives, community and spiritual leaders, and up and coming professionals. More significantly, this position exposed me to the world of entrepreneurship. I was working with and meeting people who owned and operated their own businesses and made careers out of what they loved to do. Up until this point in my life, I believed that the only way to earn a living was to get a job. I thought the only way was to work for a company or organization and climb the corporate ladder. While I know plenty of people who have been successful in corporate America and love what they do, I found that it wasn't the right fit for me.

This job consisted of documenting and celebrating the achievement of others and hosting networking events across the country. The company produced books that highlighted and shared the stories of individuals who had overcome setbacks to achieve success. The work was uplifting, inspiring, and rewarding. I was content with this new job for a while and eventually held several different positions within the company. Although I enjoyed my work and I was great at what I did, there was still a part of me that was unfulfilled. I was searching for something different, but I couldn't put my finger on it. I felt like I was supposed to be doing something different, something bigger. My passion was stirring and beginning to burn a hole inside of me. I knew there was more for me to do, and my purpose was calling my name. I was inspired by my work and sharing other people's success stories, but deep inside, I didn't feel successful. I too wanted to follow my dreams and achieve my own levels of success.

Little did I know that my position with this company was the training ground that would eventually lead me to my purpose and allow me to pursue my passions. After many years of documenting achievement and celebrating success and being exposed to such amazing examples, I began recognizing patterns and common threads between those who have accomplished their goals and achieved some level of success in their lives. I began to study and compare these journeys. What action steps did successful people take to achieve and accomplish their goals? What types of obstacles did they face and have to overcome? What were the internal and external driving forces of their success? These and many other questions began to stir in my soul and became the foundation of my coaching and motivational speaking business. It is now my mission to share these insights and patterns with as many people as possible through my coaching, speaking, and products. I created a business that allows me to use my natural gifts of speaking, being on stage, and facilitating workshops and seminars. Through my business I help others find their passion, pursue their dreams and create their own success stories.

I eventually had to stop multitasking and choose a focus. I chose in favor of my passions. I made the decision to quit that job to start my own company, to walk in my purpose and focus on my dream full time.

LESSON 15

Only You Can Define What Success Looks Like For You!

*Because I shifted gears so often, and it took me a bit longer than most to find my focus, I was labeled as a "**Jack Of All Trades, Master Of None**." Not everyone understood my dream or my passion. When I shared my vision with others, not everyone was as enthusiastic about my plans. They figured this was another one of my many ventures. They thought that I was nuts, a basket case, wishy-washy, and plain ungrateful to quit a "good" job in this economy. Regardless of the chatter going on around me, I knew I had discovered my purpose, and I had a vision. I made the right decision for me.*

Today, we hear a lot about finding your passion, living your purpose, and doing something that you love to do. When I graduated high school, this was not an option. I was told to work hard and make lots of money. No one said anything about enjoying the work that you do. Back then, there were not many tests designed to help students discover their strengths or to choose a career path that coincides with their natural gifts and talents. Today, however, there are a number of tools in the marketplace to help you narrow your focus and figure out what brings you the most joy. There are also tools books, workshops, and coaching programs to help you discover your passions.

Living your dreams does not automatically mean you have to be an entrepreneur. We are all special and unique and called to fulfill our life's purpose in many different ways. If you have the opportunity to use your natural gifts and talents, enjoy what you do, and are content with your current occupation and contribution to the world, you are where you are supposed to be. You should not feel like you are doing something wrong or missing out in some way because you have chosen to work for a company or organization rather than start your own business.

Not everyone can or should quit their job to pursue their passion full time. Depending on your passion and calling, this may not be necessary. Not everyone is designed to be an entrepreneur. You might already be in a position that brings you joy and allows you to live out your passions. Or your passion may be something that you can do in the evenings or on the weekends. There is no right or wrong way to live out your passions and fulfill your dreams. You need to be honest with yourself and be courageous enough to do what is right for you.

Furthermore, success is relative and a personal decision. You cannot measure or define your success by the world's standards or compare your journey to someone else's. Success is about more than an occupation, material possessions, and financial rewards. Success is different for every person. One person may dream of climbing the ladder and becoming a corporate CEO; another may dream of entrepreneurship and running their own empire; and yet another may dream teaching and developing our next generation of leaders.

Whether you are clear about your purpose and are already living your passions, or you have yet to figure out what you are passionate about and have not uncovered your calling, or maybe you are like I was, multitalented with no focus, wherever you are in your success journey, **Only You Can Define What Success Looks Like For You!**

MY CHOICE:
Success is not a destination; it is a journey.
I choose to achieve my personal success
and ENJOY my journey!

SELF Talk

What does success look like to you?

_____

_____

_____

What do you desire to experience in your life?

_____

_____

_____

What motivates you and brings you joy?

_____

_____

_____

What is it that you really, really, really want?

_____

_____

Do you believe you can get it?

_____

_____

_____

SELF *Talk*

YOUR CHOICE:

**You always have the power to make a new and better choice to change your life.
Moving forward, declare your choice.**

_____

_____

_____

_____

_____

_____

MY LESSONS LEARNED

Lesson #1
Your Parents Are People Too!

Lesson #2
Be You...Do You!

Lesson #3
*Where There Is Desire, Determination,
And Action...There Is Always A Way!*

Lesson #4
Whatever You Choose To Believe Is True, Is True!

Lesson #5
If Plan A Fails, Don't Be Afraid to Execute Plan B!

Lesson #6
Nothing You Ever Learn Is In Vain!

Lesson #7
Know Your Numbers!

Lesson #8
*You Alone Are Responsible For Your Happiness,
And You Can Only Change You!*

Lesson #9

Your Current Situation, Condition, Or Predicament
Does Not Define Who You Are!

Lesson #10

Live Within Your Means, And Never
Spend More Than You Make!

Lesson #11

It's Never Too Late To Live Your Dreams
And Accomplish Your Goals!

Lesson #12

Strive for Excellence!

Lesson #13

Everyone Deserves A Second Chance, Even You!

Lesson #14

We All Need Help Sometimes!

Lesson #15

Only You Can Define What Success
Looks Like For You!

AFTERWORD

*Each of us is doing the best we can do at the present moment.
If we know better, had more understanding, and awareness
then we would do it differently – Louise Hay*

Resentment, criticism, guilt and fear cause major setbacks in our lives and distorts the view we have of ourselves and the world around us. Awareness and willingness are the keys to self-improvement and personal development. When you are aware of your personal issues and willing to work on yourself, your life will improve. You become open to solutions and a different way of thinking. You forgive yourself and others and stop holding grudges. You stop blaming others for the things you have been through and what you feel is wrong with your life. You stop holding yourself hostage and open yourself up the abundant and wonderful life that God intended for each of us to live. But most importantly, you take back the power you have to change your current state and create the life that you want to live.

Luckily for us, our past does not dictate our future. No, we cannot change, erase, or redo the past. However, we can embrace it, learn from it, and continue to move forward in our lives. We can also share our journeys and allow others to borrow from our experiences and lessons learned.

Because I preach taking 100% responsibility for your life, I am often asked the following questions, *"What about those experiences that I did not cause or ask for? What about the bad things that happened to me that were out of my control? How do I take responsibility for what someone did to me?"* Yes, I agree that there are things that happened to each of us that are out of our control. I also agree, that we sometime suffer at the hands of another person. I am not condoning that or making excuses for anyone. What I do know is that we are responsible for our own choices and how we respond and react to what is done to us. So often I see people suffering because they were the victim of another person's choices or bad decisions. And that suffering affects their life and they are unable to move forward. In these cases, I believe that we still have a responsibility to help ourselves. We have a responsibility to heal and move beyond what others have done to us. Sometimes taking action steps may mean seeking counsel, professional help, and doing what is necessary to move forward in your life. When you heal and move beyond these type of circumstances, you are no longer anyone's victim and you regain your power and control of your destiny.

Thank you for allowing me to share a few of my life stories and experiences with you. Whether or not you can identify with my particular experiences, I hope that you can take my lessons learned and apply them to some area of your life and share them with someone else who needs inspiration, encouragement, and proof that there is a bright, shining light at the end of the tunnel.

Be kind to yourself! Celebrate your successes and wear your experiences proudly. Your past mistakes are meant to guide you not define you. I encourage you to love yourself and embrace your journey. If you are not exactly where you want to be in life, make new and better choices. Find your unique balance so that you have the time and energy to make necessary changes and focus on accomplishing your goals. Seek help and support. Invest in a coach, find a mentor and surround yourself with like-minded and supportive people. Be determined, steadfast, and stay focused on your goals. Be willing to make the critical moves that move you toward your goals. And finally, take action. Don't just wish and dream about something new and different. Create a plan of action to make your dreams your reality.

With the right Balance, Support, Determination, and ACTION, every dream is possible...YOUR dream is possible!

"Find Balance, Make Moves and LIVE Your Dreams!"

Do you have a DREAM or IDEA but don't know how or where to start?

I can help with the "HOW"

LIVE FIND BALANCE MAKE MOVES YOUR DREAMS

with Tamara Hartly

"With the right balance, support, determinatin, and ACTION, every dream is possible...YOUR dream is possible!"

@YourHowToCoach

Speaker, Author, Columnist, and Personal Success Coach

THANKS AND SPECIAL ACKNOWLEDGMENTS

I want to thank my husband, **_Steven Hartley, Sr._**, for being my "vice president," my best friend, and the love of my life. He always has my back and my best interest at heart. He knows me better than anyone and still loves me unconditionally. He pushes me, supports me, and shares the vision…Hartley Unlimited!

I thank my one and only "soul sister" Tia for her love and support. Our bond is thicker than blood, and when I am down, it is her sense of humor that makes me laugh out loud. I thank my brother-in-law, Jason, for understanding our special relationship and enduring the late-night phone calls and giggle sessions. To my nieces and nephews (Malika, Jason, Akira, and Ahsan), I love you all! Thanks for keeping me entertained with the funny things you do and say on a daily basis.

I thank my family, The Barnetts and The Bythewoods. Especially my grandparents (Papaw, Banny, Johne, and Joe Sr. - RIH), my sister/aunt Terry, my aunt Brenda - RIH, and all of my uncles (Kenny, Lester "Uncle Ches", Calvin - RIH, Jeff, Lawrence "Uncle Man," Frank "Grump," and John "Uncle Chrissy" - RIH, all of whom helped raise me and have always supported my endeavors. I am thankful for my many cousins, great aunts, and great uncles. Family means more to me than anything!

I am also very blessed to have many friends to share this life with (old school and new school). I appreciate your encouragement, support, laughter and tears. You hold me accountable and tell me like it "t-i-s." Trina, Melissa, Mia, Danielle, Malinda, Kellie, Inez, Marlene, Laseanda (My Twin), Valerie and Dawn, each of your friendships are unique and special.

Katrina, Dawna, Lasandra, YaYa, Khalilah, Janelle, Tammy and Charlita "Susie" (my MO crew), you always allow me to be me at all times, and you helped me laugh through some of my most difficult times.

A special shout out to Chad, who has been my self-proclaimed arch-nemesis since high school. We have a special friendship that I treasure. My life-long competition with you has pushed me to new heights. Derrik, my *"brotha' from anotha' motha'*," we are so much alike and always on one accord, always thinking of new ways to take over the world. 4.0 for life! I also thank his wife Tiffini for being my sister and supporting her husband's calling.

And, of course, I can't forget my Howard University crew: Erika, Kerri, Chassidy, Ife, Tina, Mimi, Alva, Shantell, Toya, Melody and Nakia. I love each one of you! *"Aaaaa Ooooo Aight!"*

I want to thank the Hartley Unlimited Team and everyone who helped to bring this project to fruition including my creative partners: Misty Blue Media; Pen With Purpose, and my PR glam squad Jocelyn Allen, Chandra Lewis and their incredible team at The TALA Agency. I also want to thank all of my Sisterfriends: "God's Girl" Dawn, "Lady Xtreme," "AC," Toni, "The Amazing" Tei Street, Sandra, Brandi "Záhria," Linh and Harriet for your support and for catching the vision of **Your Sisterfriends**®.

And last, but certainly not least in my heart, I want to thank my parents Esther Bythewood and Joe Bythewood Jr. I thank you both for giving me life.

Esther - I love and appreciate you! You sacrificed so much to help me live my dreams. You were the first person who ever told me that I was special and extraordinary. And I believed you because of your example. You can do so many things. Your talents and creativity are limitless, and that encouraged me to be who I am. You are truly an inspiration to me and so many others. ***You are the wind beneath my wings.*** *"And Mom, thanks for the Dragon! I would not have gotten this book out of my head without it!"*

Joe - I love you! You are a true genius. You followed your passion and made many of your dreams come true. This example has given me the courage to uncover my passions and follow my own dreams.

ABOUT THE AUTHOR

Tamara Hartley "Your How-To Coach," is a speaker, author, advice columnist and personal success coach. She helps individuals "DO THE HOW" to make their dreams their reality. Her programs and products help individuals focus and take the necessary action steps they need to take to accomplish their goals.

Tamara has over 15 years' experience coaching and developing individuals. She holds a bachelor's degree in business administration, a dual-disciplined master's degree in marketing and communication, and has studied industrial/organizational psychology, coaching psychology, personal success and personal development.

The mother of five, Tamara is married and resides with her family in Columbus, Ohio.

COACHING PROGRAMS

Tamara's coaching programs are a unique blend of coaching support and personal development. She helps individuals discover their passions and define what success looks like for them. Her tools and assessments help her clients to identify and maximize their gifts, talents, strengths and abilities and take ACTION to accomplish their goals.

Your Personal Success and "How-To" Coach
Coaching and Consulting
www.YourHowToCoach.com

ADVICE COLUMN

Tamara gives "REAL Advice from REAL Experience." She uses her personal life experiences and lessons learned to give others a different perspective to help them make critical decisions, in their lives, relationships, and careers.

Your Advice Guru (The Advice column)
www.YourAdviceGuru.com
Send questions to Advice@YourAdviceGuru.com

SPEAKING AND WORKSHOPS

Tamara has addressed professional audiences across the country and inspired entrepreneurs as the opening speaker for the world's leading motivational speaker Les Brown. Tamara can tailor a variety of speaking topics and training programs around her core message in order to meet your group or organization's exact needs and interests. When you bring Tamara into your organization you are guaranteed a lively, informational, and highly engaging program that leaves participants inspired, empowered, and motivated to make positive changes in their lives and to meet the challenges of their professional and personal lives.

Tamara teaches practical skills and strategies that can immediately be applied in the workplace and everyday life. For more information, meet Tamara at one of her websites and receive a FREE Copy of her e-book *REAL Advice from REAL Experience: Advice, Tips and Strategies for Your Life, Relationships and Career.*

Book Tamara for your next event
www.TamaraHartley.com

Websites:
www.YourHowToCoach.com (Coaching Programs)
www.YourAdviceGuru.com (Advice Column)
www.TamaraHartley.com (Official Website)

Tamara is social, stay connected:

@YourHowToCoach
on Facebook, Twitter and Instagram

How-To Videos available on YouTube

Contact Information:
Tamara Hartley
PO Box 9584
Columbus, OH 43209
800.747.0172
info@TamaraHartley.com

Visit My Websites,
Join My Mailing List
and Get a FREE copy of My E-Book

www.YourAdviceGuru.com
www.YourHowToCoach.com
www.TamaraHartley.com

BOOK CLUB QUESTIONS
FOR DISCUSSION

1. How did you experience the book? Were you engaged immediately, or did it take a while to get into it? How did you feel reading it—amused, sad, disturbed, confused, bored...?

2. If you could ask Tamara a question, what would you ask?

3. Has this book changed you—broadened your perspective? Have you learned something new or been exposed to different ideas about yourself or other people?

4. Is there any particular aspect of Tamara's life that shocked or surprised you?

5. Were there any parts of Tamara's story where you would have liked more information?

6. Were there any parts of Tamara's story that were too detailed? Which?

7. Could you relate to any parts of Tamara's story? Have you had any similar experiences?

8. Would you be embarrassed or ashamed to share your life experiences?

9. Which of your life experiences have taught you the greatest lessons?

10. Do you easily take responsibility for your decisions and actions?

11. Do you need to forgive yourself or others for something that happened in your past?

12. What are some of the labels you have worn and have had to overcome?

13. Are you quick to judge and label others based upon their life circumstances?

14. What life lesson can you pass on to others?

Tamara would love to be a part of your book club discussion. To book Tamara for a live appearance or discussion via Google Hangout or Skype please e-mail your request with complete details to: info@TamaraHartley.com

We would love to hear your feedback and your reactions to the stories in this book. Please let us know what your favorite stories were and how they affected you. Please send an e-mail to info@TamaraHartley.com

Empowering Women | Celebrating Diversity | Promoting Sisterhood

Join Your Sisterfriends in a city near you or Book Your Own Day of Empowerment

*The **Day of Empowerment with Your Sisterfriends** is designed to empower women by providing information, tools, strategies and support to help them find their unique balance, build their confidence, self-esteem, and self efficacy, help them discover their passion and purpose, and maximize their talents, strengths and abilities to accomplish their goals and live their best life!*

Dynamic Speakers | Engaging Workshops | Shots of Health & Fitness

"Regardless of race and ethnicity, women share a very special bond. We share commonalities and experiences that bond us like sisters and friendships that sustain us through difficult times and lifts us to soaring heights."

In Loving Memory of
Joe "JB Money" Bythewood Jr.
1956-2015

A renowned musician and producer.
Music was his first love and passion.
He traveled the world performing and contributing
his musical expertise to many artists.
He LIVED his dream!